PENGUIN

ALL THE WAY

JORDIN TOOTOO plays right wing for the NHL New Jersey
Devils and has also played for the Detroit Red Wings and the
Nashville Predators. Of Inuit and Ukrainian descent, he is both
the first Inuk player and the first player to grow up in Nunavut
to participate in the NHL.

STEPHEN BRUNT is currently with Sportsnet, co-host on The FAN
590's *Prime Time Sports* with Bob McCown, and contributing writer
for *Sportsnet* magazine and sportsnet.ca. Previously, he was a columnist
at *The Globe and Mail*. He is the author of the #1 national bestselling
Searching for Bobby Orr; *Gretzky's Tears*; *Facing Ali*; *The Way It Looks
from Here*; *Second to None: The Roberto Alomar Story*; and *Diamond
Dreams: 20 Years of Blue Jays Baseball*.

Feb 2017

ALL THE WAY
MY LIFE ON ICE

JORDIN TOOTOO
with Stephen Brunt

PENGUIN

an imprint of Penguin Canada Books Inc., a Penguin Random House Company

Published by the Penguin Group
Penguin Canada Books Inc., 320 Front Street West, Suite 1400, Toronto, Ontario M5V 3B6, Canada

Penguin Group (USA) LLC, 375 Hudson Street, New York, New York 10014, U.S.A.
Penguin Books Ltd, 80 Strand, London WC2R 0RL, England
Penguin Ireland, 25 St Stephen's Green, Dublin 2, Ireland (a division of Penguin Books Ltd)
Penguin Group (Australia), 707 Collins Street, Melbourne, Victoria 3008, Australia
(a division of Pearson Australia Group Pty Ltd)
Penguin Books India Pvt Ltd, 11 Community Centre, Panchsheel Park, New Delhi – 110 017, India
Penguin Group (NZ), 67 Apollo Drive, Rosedale, Auckland 0632, New Zealand
(a division of Pearson New Zealand Ltd)
Penguin Books (South Africa) (Pty) Ltd, 24 Sturdee Avenue, Rosebank, Johannesburg 2196, South Africa

Penguin Books Ltd, Registered Offices: 80 Strand, London WC2R 0RL, England

First published in Viking hardcover by Penguin Canada Books Inc., 2014

Published in this edition, 2015

6 7 8 9 10 (RRD)

Photo credits:
Tootoo playing to the Nashville fans: John Russell/Getty Images
Tootoo in a Red Wings jersey: Dave Reginek/Getty Images
All other photos courtesy of Jordin Tootoo

Manufactured in the U.S.A.

LIBRARY AND ARCHIVES CANADA CATALOGUING IN PUBLICATION

Tootoo, Jordin, 1983–, author
All the way / Jordin Tootoo.

Includes index.
Originally published by Viking, 2014.
ISBN 978-0-14-318920-6 (pbk.)

1. Tootoo, Jordin, 1983–. 2. Tootoo, Jordin, 1983– —Alcohol use.
3. Inuit hockey players—Biography 4. Hockey players—Canada--
Biography. 5. Recovering alcoholics—Canada--Biography. I. Title.

GV848.5.T66A3 2015   796.962092   C2015-900650-3

eBook ISBN 978-0-14-319310-4

Visit the Penguin Canada website at **www.penguin.ca**

Special and corporate bulk purchase rates available; please see
www.penguin.ca/corporatesales or call 1-800-810-3104.

FOR JENNIFER
FOR MY PARENTS
FOR CORINNE
FOR TERENCE

INTRODUCTION
by Joseph Boyden

I once had the chance to head far north to Rankin Inlet in Nunavut with an amazing group of people, including CBC radio icon Shelagh Rogers, Mike Stevens, one of the world's greatest harmonica players, and Jonathan Torrens, also known as J-Roc, from *Trailer Park Boys*. We were doing a community literacy event called the Peter Gzowski Invitational Golf Tournament. This was in March, 150 kilometres south of the Arctic Circle, so as you can imagine, the "golf" was actually played on a small iced-over lake, where at one point I used a frozen walrus penis for a putter.

One evening we were invited by the community to watch and participate in some traditional Inuit hand-drumming and throat singing, and it was on this night that I got to meet Jordin Tootoo's father, Barney. I remember asking to have my photo taken with Barney and he happily agreed. Clearly, he was used to the attention. After all, his NHL-playing son was the toast of

Nunavut, and much of Canada, for that matter. But what was also so clearly apparent was the deep pride and love this father had for his son. Barney's face glowed when I gushed about how Jordin was one of the league's scrappiest and most memorable players. I remember thinking to myself, "What a perfect story this is, a young indigenous kid growing up just outside the Arctic Circle, taught to play hockey by his adoring dad, and nurtured into the fit beast that he is by his equally adoring mother. Now this would make a great biography!"

It wasn't until recently, when I finished reading *All the Way*, that I realized the real power of Jordin's story. And how naive I was to ever conjure the word "idyllic."

Jordin Tootoo does not pull punches. If you already know who he is, you might smile or, more probably, grimace at this particular cliché. If you don't know Jordin, you will soon learn the story of how this kid from a remote village beat the odds to become one of the toughest men in the NHL, a league with no shortage of the world's toughest men. But this book is far from just a story about the NHL, or even hockey, although that brilliantly Canadian sport is at the heart of it.

When I say Tootoo doesn't pull punches, of course, I mean this literally. Ask anyone in the NHL who has ever dropped gloves with him. But I also mean it in the more classic sense. Jordin is ready to share the story of his life so far. And what a story it is. Does he pull *any* punches?

Ask his parents, whom he loves dearly. Ask Stephen Brunt, who so concisely and objectively and in a pitch-perfect way helped Jordin to get the words down on the page. Ask his friends or his wife or the many people he has come into contact with over his years of fame in a league where he epitomizes that rare combination of grace and brutality. Jordin's story is startling. It is at times a tough read. It can be beautiful. It is deeply tragic. It is triumphant. And not necessarily in that order. This book is a roller-coaster ride, the rise and fall and rise of a young man with all of the cards stacked against him, who manages to carve out a place for himself in one of the most vied-for and difficult professional sports positions in the world.

Let's talk for a moment about the odds he faced: the son of an Inuit father and white mother, Jordin Tootoo was raised in that isolated and largely Inuk community of Rankin Inlet in Nunavut. Most professional hockey players are groomed from the time that they first step on the ice as little children to play in highly organized and competitive leagues. There's no such thing as that in Rankin Inlet. Jordin didn't play true organized hockey until well into his teens, a fact that seems near impossible to coaches and scouts. Jordin learned his craft and his skills on that same small frozen lake where I batted around golf balls with a walrus phallus as well as on an indoor rink where his father played house league and coached Jordin and his older brother, Terence. In a league like the NHL, where size certainly does matter and players are typically well over six feet and tough guys are often much bigger than that, Jordin tops out at five foot ten. Imagine stepping onto the ice and going toe-to-toe with enforcers who tower above you and whose job is to knock your head off, and yours, theirs. But Jordin has certainly never backed down from a fight and most typically wins them. In short, Jordin breaks the rules in terms of his physical stature, but his incredible speed and strength have more than made up for that.

The most daunting odds stacked against him, though, are that Jordin grew up in a home seized by the throes of alcohol addiction and the fear, anger, and violence that comes with that. His upbringing was far from ideal, to say the least. Simply to emerge from that home intact is a triumph, not to mention how Jordin has become a role model for youth facing the same odds.

But before he found sobriety, Jordin knew how to party. Yes, hockey players are famous for this, but Jordin took it to a whole new level. That he was able, for years, to drink to such excess on a regular basis that blackouts were a part of life and still get up and not just function but dominate on the rink might have been some of the biggest odds he managed to beat. In so many ways, Jordin Tootoo is a walking, talking, brawling, honest, open, and vulnerable contradiction, a man who by all accounts should never, on the surface, have made it out of Rankin Inlet.

Yet Jordin's is not a story of some kid's incredible luck of escaping a home and community wracked by deep trouble. Quite the opposite. He knows where he comes from and rather than having abandoned it, he embraces his world. Nunavut is home. Jordin is a product and a vital part of Rankin Inlet, and certainly of Nunavut, a world that indeed has its problems but also has a far more deep-rooted power. The Inuit are a people of the land. As much as Jordin's father faces off with his own demons in tow, Barney was and remains an incredibly skilled Inuk of the land, a place where he never drinks but instead teaches others the skills not just to survive but also to flourish in the world's toughest physical climate and terrain.

Let me bring you back to that visit to Rankin I made a few years ago. When Barney found out I wanted to get out on the land, he arranged for a couple of his friends to take me by snowmobile to hunt ptarmigan. As we left town, we passed racks of pink Arctic char and seal meat, even a polar bear hide hanging to dry in the cold sun and wind. And it wasn't very far out that I realized how easy it would be to become lost in this white landscape, the only markers some stone rises and a couple of scattered inukshuks.

That afternoon I watched in awe as these new friends led me through a landscape in which I often became disoriented, and we were never, I'm sure, more than ten or twenty kilometres from town. In fact, at one point in the afternoon when I was feeling like I had a grip on things, I split off from the main party on my snowmobile, only to realize twenty minutes later that I had lost any of the other tracks and the rise I thought was my way back turned out not to be. All I could do was sit and wait for one of the Inuk hunters to follow my trail out and find me as I watched the wind blow snow across my trail and the sun sink ever faster to dusk. It was then I realized the harsh beauty of this place is matched only by the sheer brutal and crushing weight of the land's relentless neutrality when it comes to whether or not a puny human lives or dies on its back. And so we puny humans, if we hope to live in such a world, need to learn it from birth and never be so foolish as to make a major mistake. This is the world where Jordin's father excels, and this is the world where Jordin, too, feels most at home.

While reading his memoir, I came to understand something vital. Jordin inherently understands that the daunting man that he is both on and off the ice is directly attributed to his connection to the land. And so maybe it is no miracle at all that Jordin not just survives but flourishes on the ice of an arena because he learned to do the same on the frozen muskeg of home.

This autobiography is not a story that asks the reader to pity Jordin, and it is never a book that attempts to explain or make excuses for anything. I don't think I've ever before read such an honest, bare, and exposed account of a life. One doesn't expect someone in his position as a tough and brash tool of incitement on the ice to open up and be so vulnerable on the page. Perhaps this is what proves to me that Jordin Tootoo is the strongest person I've ever come across (with the possible exception of heavyweight boxing champ George Chuvalo, a man whose family I grew up with and who, in the depth of tragedy, has done much the same as Jordin in opening up to others and speaking out against the dangers of addiction). Jordin really is incredibly brave. In this book he truly bares himself, a trait not typical for most any man, especially one who has played in the world's toughest league for a decade.

Will this book cause some shock waves, not just within Jordin's family and community but also across our country? I believe it will. Part of healing is not just being able to admit to your own shortcomings but also to the shortcomings of those around you, in the hopes that this admission might help to point out a more healthy direction. I'm blown away by Jordin's matter-of-fact approach to his difficult upbringing and how it directly affected his own health and well-being as a young man. Jordin is a man who doesn't believe in wasting his words. Like his hockey, though, his words are fierce, they are carefully considered, and they will knock you on your ass with their sniper's ability to hit their mark. After all, Jordin is not just one of the league's great fighters. He also has one of the league's most powerful slapshots.

This cut-to-the-bone philosophical approach he takes to where he found himself then and where he finds himself now is deeply aboriginal. I made the startling realization after finishing his book that he is so much like the characters I explore in my fiction: tough men, world-weary and careful with their words, men who not only watch their surroundings closely but tap into them. But as soon as you scratch the surface, you find people straining for answers, straining for justice and understanding and for the truth just below. Jordin has done something my characters were never able to do, though: express himself so openly and with such a simple honesty that you can't turn your attention away.

I'll admit I became a bit obsessed with the man after reading his book. I didn't want the story to end. And so I did what any twenty-first-century person does to find out more: I googled him. There are plenty of YouTube videos that capture his epic speed and scoring ability and especially his punishing fighting skills. It becomes obvious pretty fast why he's one of the more contentious players in the NHL. But it was a video of him speaking with Michael Landsberg on TSN's *Off the Record* about fighting that made me realize the deep intelligence, the careful consideration, and the good politician's poise when faced with tough questions. Jordin freely admitted that he's a man of few words, that he lets his actions on the ice speak for him. And yet he masterfully defended what he does and how he's perceived in some quarters while at the same time speaking with a glint in the eye and a sincerity that makes you want to like the guy. You can tell that below the calm exterior there's a depth of character earned from a lot of experience, a lot of pain and tragedy. And that kind of experience can destroy a person pretty quickly. He refuses to let it. He clearly fights as hard off the ice as he does on it to balance what his life so far has thrown at him, including the suicide of his older brother and best friend, Terence. Maybe that's what Jordin is fighting for. His brother's memory, his brother's shot at the big leagues scuttled by a bad decision one night when he thought he'd messed things up beyond repair. I won't speak for Jordin, though. He speaks for himself just fine in these pages, with a minimalist grace that begs us to read between the lines. He is nothing if not charismatic. And that charisma is born from the life he has led thus far, from the land, from his parents, from the memory of his brother that lives inside him.

Eventually, when I got to talk to the man himself, I was even more impressed by his carefully measured words and his thoughtfulness. Of course his play has thrilled me since his games with the Team Canada juniors. What a story! An Inuit kid becoming the first of his people to play in the NHL. An artist on the ice whose grace and speed match his fists of fury. Jordin Tootoo from the beginning is a truly epic Canadian story. There's no doubt about it. And just under the surface of this recounting of a life so far is the release of past burdens so that this man might move forward with true dignity.

Perhaps when Jordin does finally decide to hang up his professional hockey skates years from now, he'll choose something that both surprises and doesn't at all. Keep in mind that one of the toughest men in the NHL also travels great distances to speak to youth across Nunavut about the importance of finishing high school and of understanding that if you can imagine your dream, if you can see it in your head, then you simply have to pursue it with a doggedness that does in fact challenge the odds stacked against all of us. His message is at once simple and complex; it is both artful and tough; it is highly sensible yet so highly lofty that many youth must feel he's asking them to do the impossible. But just watch him on the internet speaking to these youth and you can see the awe, the deep appreciation in their eyes. His straightforward words brim over with truth.

Maybe Jordin will eventually choose politics. It's not that far-fetched. He has the charisma, he has the respect of his people, he has both the message and the real-life experience to back what he says, and his family certainly has their fair share of politicians. Jordin's father, Barney, while he holds no official title, is certainly considered a "chief" in his community of Rankin Inlet. Jordin's uncle was a Speaker of the Legislative Assembly of Manitoba, and Jordin's cousin was a Speaker of the Legislative Assembly of Nunavut. Or perhaps I'm just projecting my expectations and desires on him. I'm certainly not the only one who does so. Time will tell what path he takes next, but what's sure in my mind is that he'll apply the same work ethic, the same single-minded focus and will that he always has.

The title of this book, *All the Way*, might be one of the most telling and personal aspects of Jordin's autobiography. These words come from Terence, jotted down in what became his last note to his younger sibling, urging him not to give up and to always look after their family. "Go all the way." At once a simple statement, it also carries the weight of their world together. "Take care of the family. You are the man." And with those few words, Jordin was left alone in what should have been the greatest year of his life, having not long before that been drafted into the NHL.

Like I say, this is a devastating story, it is a triumphant story, it is a story of succeeding despite the odds, the first act in the tale of a very special man who is as controversial as he is enigmatic. Yes, he is an agitator and an enforcer, but more importantly, he is a truly gifted hockey player. More importantly still, Jordin Tootoo is an Inuk. He is the son of his father; he is the son of his mother; he is a survivor. And if you will allow me to speak it out loud: Jordin Tootoo has the gift of the warrior poet inside him. Like much of my favourite writing, this story, on the surface, is simply told. But it carries the weight of thousands of years on the land. It carries the weight of great victory and even greater loss. But what it truly promises is that there's so much more to come.

Joseph Boyden
Paris, France
June 2014

*T*he sun has been up for a long time, though the truth is it barely sets in high summer. The others are still sound asleep in a ten foot–by–ten foot cabin, a bare-bones wooden box on the shores of a northern lake in the middle of a landscape I am struggling to absorb. The sky and the water are deep blue. The brownish tundra unfolds endlessly in all directions, broken only by huge boulders. It is silent, absolutely silent, save for the whistling wind, which never seems to die completely, a blessing when it keeps the clouds of mosquitoes at bay, and for the occasional squawks of the huge storks that spend their summers here. Beyond that, there are no real signs of life, except for the Great Horned Owl we saw perched on a rock during the long, rough ride in on quads. Somewhere not so far away a grizzly bear has been spotted heading in our general direction, and so even on a short stroll a rifle is necessary, though the truth is, with me packing, the bear has absolutely nothing to fear.

We are here—my son Nathaniel and me; Jordin Tootoo; his father, Barney; and his young nephew Terence, named after a brother and son lost—to fish for giant lake trout. The water is so clear you can watch the fish chase the lure back to the boat, though it's not so easy to convince them to bite. We cast for hours and hours. We pause occasionally to eat from the mixed bag of goodies packed in the grub box: kielbasa sausage, peanut butter cookies, all manner of snacks, plus traditional Inuit country food—air-dried char that Jordin's mother, Rose, caught and prepared and that is a delicate orange-pink and retains the subtle taste of the sea, and muktuk, the layer of blubber found just beneath the skin of a beluga whale and the kind of thing you serve to southerners just to see how they'll react. It's extraordinarily chewy and doesn't taste like much of anything, which may explain why the preferred method of preparation, after methodically cutting each tiny strip, is to smother it in China Lily soy sauce.

"We are going out on the land," Jordin told me shortly after we first met. "So you can understand." You miss it the first few times, the article in that sentence, but eventually you come to understand its profound significance. Not "our" land, because here that is self-evident, but "the" land. It has no borders, other than the arbitrary political lines drawn around the territory of Nunavut, which was carved out of the larger Northwest Territories in 1999. The vast tracts above the treeline, not just here but in northern Quebec, Alaska, the tip of Labrador, and Greenland, are the domain of the Inuit people, and for them, possession and sovereignty have never been a matter of debate.

Neither is being "on the land" the same thing as camping, or fishing, or hunting, though it involves sleeping rough, catching fish, and being prepared at all times to kill whatever useful beast or bird might come along. It's not a recreation. It's holistic. It's living. And although back in the town of Rankin Inlet there are all the conveniences of modern life—the internet and satellite television and grocery stores selling all manner of food at inflated northern prices, not to mention a Tim Hortons—it's out here, on the land, where life is lived as it has been for centuries.

After the rest of the group wakes—the southerners have slept wrapped in their outdoor clothes, shivering, while the Inuit have slept stripped down to their underwear, sweating—Barney Tootoo surveys the horizon as we motor down the lake in our boat. He points to stone markers on a hillside. "That's where the caribou herds come down to cross," he says. Later, he spots a lone caribou in profile, standing on a distant rise. A rifle is readied and the caribou is put in the crosshairs, but it's too far away to take a shot.

We cruise farther along the lake and Barney points to a stone inukshuk, which may have been assembled there five days ago, or five years ago, or five hundred years ago. Its meaning, though, is clear to him. In this bay, which to my eyes looks identical to myriad other bays we have sailed right by, somewhere in time someone experienced good fishing. We drop anchor and within five minutes a twenty-pound laker is flopping around on the floor of the boat.

As the air begins to cool in late afternoon, though the sun is still high and bright in the sky, Terence finds a warm place to nap tucked inside the boat's bow. Jordin stays outside, scanning the water, casting for fish over and over again, following his father's lead, every moment one of learning, of reading the landscape, of greater understanding. How often has this scene been repeated with other fathers and other sons, stretching back to when men first arrived here?

Jordin was right. This is where the story begins. On the land. This is where it has to start.

Stephen Brunt

ONE

On the land is where you understand how simple life is. It really brings you back down to earth. It's so humbling and so peaceful. You go to Toronto or New York and everything is moving at a hundred miles an hour. You come up here and you put your phone away and nothing else matters. You are in the moment. You have to be.

When you're out on the land and meet people out there, it doesn't matter if our families are feuding back in town. Out there you help each other out. All of that other stuff is left behind. It's like when I go to the rink and I leave everything at the door. I leave all of my personal issues outside when I walk into the arena. It's the same as here—when you go out on the land, you leave everything behind, all of your fricking problems.

The land is my dad's getaway. He's my go-to guy because he knows how life is out there. That's his comfort zone. When I go out with my buddies it's awesome, but it's not the same as being with my dad. You don't have that same sense of peace. My dad always knows what's going on.

We first went out on the land when my brother, Terence, and I were little kids. My mom used to go too, but now she's not all that gung-ho about it. She likes going to our cabin, which is a fifteen- or twenty-minute quad ride from the house, where we net the char, but really going out on the land is my dad's thing. His parents lived out on the land until probably halfway through their lives. They would follow the caribou herds. Then they moved into the community in Churchill, Manitoba.

These days, people don't actually live out on the land full time, but in the spring they will go out for a month to camp when the weather is nice. In the winter it's just too harsh. I couldn't imagine what it was like fifty, sixty, or seventy years ago, when they were actually living out there all year round.

Being out here is part of our culture and lifestyle in the north. You go out with people who know the land and eventually, as time goes on, you learn the ropes—and you have to learn, or you'll get into trouble. In summer, if you go off the trail, you won't know where you're going unless you remember landmarks. That's what people do when they go out hunting. In the winter, it's totally different. The landscape and the landmarks that you see in summer have disappeared under the snow. You lose your sense of direction. You can get lost just like that. People get lost all the time—people who don't know the territory. They say they're going out hunting for the day, the day turns into two, and then search-and-rescue has to get out there to find them. A storm can just turn around on you within hours.

I don't really care to go hunting or fishing down south because it's not like it is here.

When I say "hunting and fishing," people envision going to a camp where dinner's served and you have a guide and everything's taken care of. They don't understand how tough it is here, that you're on your own. Like that caribou we saw. You may want to shoot a caribou, but then you have to deal with the fucking mosquitoes and cutting it up and hauling it out. Your regular hunter down south has people to do that for him.

When my buddy Scottie Upshall came up here, I told him we're going to jump on the quad and go fishing. For him, jumping on the quad meant riding on a road, a paved road, for a couple of hours nice and easy, because that's what they know down south. It's not that you break your own trail and it's hard. I think it came as a bit of a shock to him, getting knocked around like that.

When I was a kid, as much as I loved the fishing and hunting, the best part was all the other shit we had to do: packing up, making camp, unpacking, tying everything up. That's really hard work, but for my dad it's just second nature. You tie everything up and when you think it's tied well enough, he tells you it's not because he knows how rough it is out there. Knowing those little things, that's what I really admire about my father—that he has all those skills and that survival mindset. I think that's how I learned to go into survival mode when I'm out on the ice. That comes from all the trouble I've seen out on the land growing up, because even when things are going okay, something bad is going to happen eventually and you've always got to prepare for it. Out on the land, you never know.

MY PEOPLE, the Inuit people, are very humble. And they work together. When times are tough, they depend on each other. As an Inuk person, when I go home and look at our elders, I know that life is very simple for them. As long as they have their traditional foods and culture around them, life is good. All of this other materialistic stuff means nothing. I think that's what's great about being an Inuk. Whatever is put in front of you, you deal with it and go from there. For my family, everything has always been pretty simple. We don't need a nice car and we don't need the best Ski-Doo to be all flashy and be the cool guys. Up here, being a good hunter and a good family guy is all that matters.

I come from a mixed race family, but there's not a lot of talk about that in Rankin Inlet. A lot of white people come up here for jobs. It's the same in a lot of the remote communities. Race is less and less of an issue because there are white people who have lived here for generations. Here, you are really defined more by your surroundings. A lot of white people move up north, people who have grown up in well-off families and had everything given to them. They come here and it kind of brings them back to earth. They start to realize that what is most important is living a simple life and being able to provide for your family. That's why knowing the land, going out hunting and fishing, and knowing the tradition of living the Inuit lifestyle are more important than race. At the end of the day, people who move up north from down south aren't going to change how life is up north because that's simply reality. Instead, they have to become Inuit in their own way. They've got to live the Inuit lifestyle or the community isn't going to accept them.

When I was growing up, I can remember meeting my dad's co-workers and buddies who had moved here from places like Newfoundland. Every time we'd go out hunting or fishing, they were always welcome. I remember waking up on Saturdays and Dad's white co-workers would be waiting outside our house at seven in the morning to go out on the land. My dad wouldn't go run after them. He'd say, "We're leaving at 7:30 tomorrow morning. If you're there, you're there. If not, come out and find me on the land." The white guys didn't know the land, so they were always there waiting. But after a few years of being guided, they would be comfortable enough to go out on the land by themselves, hunting and fishing and doing all that traditional stuff.

Some people also use the land as an escape from their lives, from their husbands or wives and whatever troubles they have at home. When families are feuding—husbands and uncles and aunties—they say, *Fuck, I'm going out on the land.* You know that when people get angry and go out on the land, if they don't look after themselves you may never see them again. Once you get out of town you're in the wilderness and you never know what could happen, especially if you're distracted by anger.

Sometimes, when things are getting tense at home, my dad will take off and be missing for a day, or two days. I can't imagine what it's like for my mom when my dad goes out on the land and says he's coming back in a couple of days and a storm brews up. She must be sitting at home wondering if he's coming back at all. And sometimes my dad being away is a good thing. It's a relief. She needs him to come back and take care of the family, but at the same time at least when he's out on the land, there's peace at home. That's when my mother is most peaceful—when my dad is gone. I think that's the way it is with a lot of families around here.

MY DAD WAS BORN out on the land in a little shack near Pistol Bay. His mother, Jenny Tootoo—her Inuk name was Pinwatha—was alone when he was born. There wasn't even a midwife. She tied off the umbilical cord with a piece of string and cut it with a razor blade. He was the fourth of her eleven children.

Jenny's husbands were away trapping when my dad was born. Yes, *husbands*—two of them. It was a different kind of family, though up here it wasn't so unusual. There's a book called *When the Foxes Ran* that was written by Gerry Dunning; you can buy it at the Eskimo Museum in Churchill. One of the chapters is about my grandmother and her husbands, Bob Hickes and Pierre Tootoo. Hicks was white. Tootoo—my father's father—was an Inuk, and so was Jenny. Her marriage with Pierre Tootoo was arranged when she was a baby. She met Bob Hickes, who was much older, after she was already married to Pierre, when the two men became hunting and trapping partners. The funny thing is, it was Hickes, the white man, who really taught Pierre to trap. In their home, they didn't speak English—only Inuktitut.

Here's what it says in the book:

Jenny was in love with Bob Hickes and to a lesser degree with Pierre Tootoo. The two men never fought with one another, never argued, and looked after each other as well as Jenny. All provided security to each other and the children. "It never mattered to me what father the children had, nor did it bother each father. All of our children have been equally important to us." She states, "All of them have given us happiness inna my heart and inna their hearts. What is inna your heart is what is important. I've had the love for two men. We three worked together to keep each other happy, at times even alive. Our family has never been rich, but our family has always been happy!"

My dad's family moved to Churchill, Manitoba, in 1950, not long after he was born. They lived in an area called The Flats, along the Churchill River. The men went to work at an army base there, and for the first time the children went to school. When they first moved there, they were the only Inuit family living in town. That's where my father grew up.

MY MOTHER, ROSE, is Ukrainian. She grew up on a farm just outside of Dauphin, Manitoba. So I guess that makes me a Ukimo. I know that's not the politically correct way to say it, but I like it.

Mom was an only child. From what I know, her family isn't very close, so she didn't grow up with a lot of people around her. We were never really exposed to her side of the family. They were down south, mainly in Winnipeg and Ontario. We made a few trips down to meet them, but growing up I don't ever recall us being close to her side of the family. I can remember one time when our Baba—my mother's grandmother—passed away and the funeral was in Winnipeg. Obviously, all of the kids and family went down for that. It turned into a bit of a gong show. Everything started to come out from all of the old family feuds. I was a young teenager then and I remember walking out of the ceremony at the church because it got out of control. People were arguing about all kinds of things—I'm not sure if it was the will, who did or didn't deserve what, but it was a mess—so me and my brother and my dad actually walked out of the funeral.

My parents met back in the day; Dad went down south to work and brought Mom back up north. All of these white guys were coming up north and stealing all the Inuit women, so my dad said, *Fuck you, guys, I'm going south and grabbing myself a white girl*, and he picked up this blondie. That's his story and he says he's sticking to it. I think, for Mom, it was a way to get out of her own situation. She left and basically never went back. She jumped on a plane with a fricking stranger, this little Eskimo guy trawling around. They moved to Churchill first, where Dad was from, and then later made their way north to Rankin Inlet.

What must have attracted her was my dad's personality, and I guess the way he carried himself. He's a very quiet guy when he's sober, keeps very much to himself. He goes about his own business. And then obviously he is also a cool guy and a party guy. Maybe that part of him helped take my mom's friendship with him to the next level. He's fun, he's popular, and he's a good hunter—which, back then, was how you survived and how you fed the family, so it really mattered.

But Mom was coming to a completely different universe and a different culture. I've never really asked her what kept her here, but Mom and Dad hit it off right away and had my sister, Corinne, at a young age and then went on and had my brother, Terence, and me.

Eventually, my mother's parents moved to Churchill to be closer to us. That's where my grandfather died. My grandmother worked as a baker for one of the hotels there. Later, after my grandfather passed away, she moved to Baker Lake, which is close to Rankin Inlet, and cooked in a hotel there. She was the best grandma. She sent us goodie packages of her cinnamon rolls, cookies, and doughnuts. It was always a great occasion for our family when we would get these packages. I definitely remember that.

My grandma also provided an escape for us. When there were bad fights between my mother and my father happening in our house, we kids and my mother would jump on a plane and fly to my grandma's place in Churchill or Baker Lake and stay with her for the weekend.

AS I SAID, my dad is a great guy, and on the land is where I love him the most. On the land is where I see my dad at his finest. He's fucking unbelievable. He's like a guru, the guy who understands everything in this part of the world. And when he comes down south, people just love him. He's a charming guy. He's a great, great community guy—everything you could imagine and want in a guy living up north. He has all these good qualities.

But there is another side to my dad, a flip side, a dark side that most people never see because it only comes out behind closed doors. It's like he's bipolar. When you're in Rankin Inlet, booze is around and it's just like he's a totally different man. My dad never brings booze out on the land. Out there, shit can turn on you just like that and if you're not thinking straight, your life could be in danger. But when we're home it's like a switch turns off. In a perfect world he'd just stay out there, sober, and not have to worry about a fucking thing. But the truth is, even when we were kids, he'd get out there for a couple of days and then he'd start to get the itch. He couldn't wait to get back to the house. It would be Sunday, four o'clock in the afternoon, and he would want to get home and have some cocktails because he hadn't had any in a couple of days.

Alcohol is the drug of choice in Rankin Inlet, but if you're visiting from the outside you would never know it. Technically, it's a dry town. There aren't any bars, other than the Legion, where you have to be a member, and there isn't a liquor store. So drinking isn't a social activity, with people going out together, the way it is in the south. To get booze you have to order it in, and that takes time and it's expensive. Or you can bring it in—or have somebody bring it in for you—on the plane, which is kind of under the table. So the drinking takes place in homes, with the doors closed. You're partying, but you're isolated. And it is binge drinking, drinking whatever booze is available when it's available.

My mother drinks with my father. And back when I was drinking, Terence and I would be right there with them. In those days, I didn't see the problem. Now I understand. But my parents don't understand what I see because they're stuck in this cloud. I'm not here to change people's ways because of what I went through. It's up to them to do it. When I come home now, my parents wonder why I'm not around the house half the time I'm here. It's because they're fricking boozing and I'm not going to sit around and watch that. They just don't get it. They're set in their own ways. You can't teach an old dog new tricks. Sometimes they try to hide the drinking from me, but, of course, I know what's going on.

I love my dad when we're away from this whole commotion. But sitting in the house, it's like he's just counting down the hours until I leave so he can have a few drinks. That's when I feel sorry for my mom, but at the same time, they're in it together and they're both stuck in that trap.

I know that the moment I walk out of the house, it all starts up again.

TWO

*I*n the centre of Rankin Inlet, nestled between the school and the rink, is a large pond called Williamson Lake. In summer, it is an unremarkable patch of water, but in winter, it becomes something else entirely, even on days when the wind is howling off Hudson Bay, when the temperature never creeps above forty degrees below zero. The local kids also play in the arena, where there is no need for artificial cooling to create the ice surface during the winter, and play road hockey on the snow-covered gravel streets, but it is here, outdoors, where they gather in the time-honoured Canadian tradition after classes are done, lace up their skates, and divide into teams for games of shinny. This is where Jordin Tootoo's hockey journey began, and it is where he developed his rough-and-tumble, high-energy style. In the National Hockey League, his style is distinctive, but among the kids in Rankin Inlet it's the only way to play the game.

Growing up in a small town, everyone knows everyone—and everyone knows everyone's kids. You're only a ten-minute snowmobile ride from anywhere in town and others' doors are always open. I remember leaving school and just roaming around town. Our parents weren't worried about anyone trying to kidnap us or do harm to us or anything like that. Kids have way more freedom up there than they do down south. After school, we would just scatter. We'd find different creative things to do.

Nowadays, kids have toys. To us, "toys" was making a tunnel or a fort. We would have snowball fights or go sliding, do spontaneous things. I never played video games—still don't to this day. In those days, there was no satellite TV like they have now in the north. To us, fun was being outside when it was minus forty and just going where the wind took us. That was being a kid. There was so much freedom. Down south, kids are on a pretty tight schedule. It seems like everyone is on a schedule down there. Up north, it's a free-for-all. That's something I'd love my own kids to experience some day—being able to explore the world and not have to worry.

Of course, it wasn't quite so simple when we went home. When your family has problems, you don't really want to be around the house, especially on Friday or Saturday nights when the booze starts to flow. I wonder now how many of my buddies' families were the same as mine. They didn't seem to want to go home either. It seemed like a lot of kids were always out. Were they in the same boat as I was? We never talked to each other about it. Nothing was ever said. I just remember that if friends wanted to come over to my place, I would always try to find a way to go to somebody else's place instead. Or I'd say, "Let's play road hockey for another hour under the street lights." Anything to put off walking through that door.

On a Friday night, it would be nine or ten o'clock and Mom or Dad would be yelling out the window: "Get your ass in here!" Little stuff would set them off. For instance, every year in springtime, the snow would be melting and there would be water everywhere. Of course, kids want to play in the water, and when you play in the water you get soakers—water inside your boots. And every time I got a soaker, it was like, *Holy shit, I'm going to get slapped.* I'd walk in the house and try to hide it, but they would always find out and then I'd get knocked around. I don't know what the reasoning was—that they had to do more laundry, I guess. It's one of those things that I dreaded.

I can look back and laugh about it now. It was just a frigging soaker. Why are you so pissed off about it? But if you're not in the right mental state, every little thing pisses you off. Anything your kids do. Maybe your booze order didn't come on a Friday night and you're pissed off because you don't have your fix. So you're going to take it out on your kids. Little things like that.

At least we always had hockey as an escape. After school, guys would pick up their sticks when word got around town that there was a street hockey game—guys like Pujjuut Kusugak and Warren Kusugak, who were Terence's best friends. Then after dinner we would go to the arena and hang out. There would be men's hockey or midget or bantam. We were kind of rink rats.

My dad would play at 8:30 or 9:00 at night with the

old-timers. I would go to the rink with him and watch how they laced up their skates or taped their shin pads so I could copy it. When I go home now and I'm in the dressing room in Rankin Inlet, the kids are all watching me in the same way—*see how he puts this on this way, or tapes his stick that way?* I chuckle watching them, because once upon a time that was me.

The truth is, in hockey terms and maybe in all terms, I'm a fucking long shot. I'm from Nunavut. We don't have hockey leagues. We don't have scouts coming up here. It was like a crazy fantasy that anyone from here would ever play in the NHL. When we were playing street hockey with all of our buddies or playing on the lake, we said the same things that other Canadian kids say: "I'm going to be Wayne Gretzky. I'm going to be Doug Gilmour." Because we watched *Hockey Night in Canada* and we knew all of the players. But the chance of that actually happening was almost zero.

In Nunavut, your goal is to survive one day at a time. It's a harsh environment. Your living conditions are not the greatest and you have to be fucking tough to live in the Arctic. I mean, we were playing hockey in forty below or fifty below like it was nothing. That's what we were used to. You don't see kids down south even going to school when it's forty below. Up north, the only time you don't go to school is if it's a blizzard out and you can't see ten feet in front of you.

You could see that mentality in the way we played hockey. Usually, guys who dominate in kids' hockey are bigger than the others. But the way we grow up in the north, I believe that, genetically, we're mentally tougher and physically stronger because of our living conditions. From the time I was thirteen, I would wake up at six o'clock in the morning to shovel snow at all the government buildings. Shovelling snow and working outside doing whatever: it's physically demanding. I became so much stronger, naturally stronger. I didn't realize that I was doing weights by shovelling snow. My upper body and my legs got bigger; I had all the physical strength I needed. It was natural for me. It was just how we lived.

Thank God I had an older brother, because that's who pushed me. Being three years younger than Terence and all of his buddies, I wanted to be like them and play like them. They were always hard on me. They said, "If you want to play with us you've got to do it this way." I was kind of like the guinea pig in the dressing room. They used to make me run into the boards at 100 miles an hour and then fucking laughed at me—like, "You stupid idiot, get back up and just battle through it." But I didn't mind that at all because I looked up to my brother and his buddies. I think that was the turning point in terms of becoming mentally strong and having the will to battle.

Terence would always tell me that if I wanted to play with the older guys, he would back me up—but he wasn't going to baby me. I had to fight for my ground. It started when I was this little guy—six, seven, eight years old. Even then, I had to be fricking tough. If you knocked me down, I got up. I had to get back up because I wanted to be with them, to be with these older guys that I idolized. If that hadn't happened, I wouldn't be the player I am today or the person I am today. I became fearless. When I went down south, I was always tougher and meaner than the other kids. I was a fucking maniac. That's why today I'll fucking take on a guy who's six foot six. It's mind over matter. That's all because of how I grew up.

My dad had a hockey background, so he kind of coached me and my brother and all of our friends. Dad played senior hockey in Manitoba and he was a stud. I remember watching him play in rec hockey tournaments in Rankin Inlet when we were growing up. Everyone would say, "Watch out for Barney Tootoo." I was at the rink all the time and I enjoyed watching him play. He was the best player there.

As a coach, Dad was a bit of a hard-ass. In his mind, if you want to fucking play, you've gotta fucking battle. You would get shit on, even at a young age, for doing something stupid. I probably wouldn't be a good coach because I have some of the same mentality, thinking that you've got to fight through adversity because that's what I went through. Kids nowadays, they're just pussies. Their coach tells them off or whatever and they just bow their heads and just fucking crumble.

My dad mostly coached my brother and his buddies. He couldn't coach two teams at once, so I was coached by someone else unless I was playing with the older guys. As a hockey parent, he was never the father sitting in the stands yelling—and I wasn't a player who looked at my dad in the stands and got orders from him. It always happened after the game. He'd come up to me and say, "Why did you do this? What's wrong with you? You know better." After every game, you knew that if you'd fucked up a few times, you were going to hear about it. That was actually a great way to parent a hockey kid. Dad wasn't overprotective.

His approach was more that you had to do your own thing and figure it out.

On the other hand, my mom was a yeller. Everyone knew when Rose Tootoo was in the arena because she was always screaming and yelling. If anyone touched me, she would fricking flip out.

We practised on Mondays and Thursdays and scrimmaged against each other on Saturdays. There were fifteen kids, so we just split the group in half. There weren't enough players for real teams. In peewee, there wasn't supposed to be any hitting, but my dad allowed it when he was coaching: "Boys, if you want to fuck around, battle it out." Some of the parents would say, "Geez, what are you doing, Barney?" And my dad would say, "I'm coaching them. I'm teaching them to play hockey." Because that's what hockey was to him.

Kudos to my dad for allowing us to play the game whenever he was available, but the truth is it was kind of on his own timetable, when he wasn't grabbing a drink. He'd say stuff like, "I'm only gonna drink on Tuesday this week, so on Wednesday I'll be good to go with the boys."

In the 1980s, Dad managed the local rink, so he was around all the time. We knew he was going to be there after school, so we could go to the rink any time we wanted and slap on our skates. And then after we left home, he stopped coaching. I don't know when everything fell apart between Rankin Inlet minor hockey and my dad. He just kind of disappeared from hockey after we left home. He did his duties managing at the rink, but then I guess he didn't want to have to deal with kids anymore, so he kind of drifted away. Kids are always asking him to coach them, but he won't do it now.

When you're young, you should enjoy hockey, you should have fun, and that's what we did. Our parents didn't put us on a specific regimen. We wouldn't shoot pucks all day to be the next Wayne Gretzky. Nowadays, kids are training twelve months a year and by the time they're teenagers they're fucking done with hockey because their parents pushed them through all of this shit for twelve months a year and didn't give them a break. We played on natural ice, from the middle of November until May, when the snow came down from the arena roof. Once the ice had melted, we played baseball or soccer. To this day, in the off-season I put my gear away for a month and don't even look at it, because you want to miss the game a little bit. Growing up, that's how we did it. In the summer, we were out fishing and hunting and playing other sports. When I go home now, I tell the kids that as much as we love the game, you need time away from it.

There are a lot of great hockey players in the north. You see all of these young, talented kids and they're unreal until their teenaged years, and that's when women and booze come into the picture and it changes their whole outlook. There's your love and passion for the game, but then you have to deal with a whole new element and, for a lot of them, hockey takes second place.

For me, I knew hockey was always going to be my life. My goal was to play in the NHL, even though that was a crazy idea for a kid from Rankin Inlet. A big part of that goal was sticking with it, even when it would have been easier to stay home and be a local superstar. A lot of kids who leave the north to go play Triple A hockey end up going home for these stupid tournaments and never leaving, all because for one weekend they were the stars of the show. Growing up, they were always the best player and then down south they realize that they're just an average kid. That's how it was for me, but I always had my dad saying, "No, you've got to stay down there and just work through it."

Between the ages of seven and twelve we played hockey only with our friends, and then at peewee and bantam ages, we moved into organized hockey. Terence and I were the ones who stood out. We would go to tournaments in other communities and we were always the talk of the town. We were always kind of counted on to be the difference-makers. To me, it just kind of came naturally. I was a good skater. I wasn't the biggest guy out there, but mentally I knew how to battle through. The truth is, I was skating around other kids, but I didn't feel like that because my peers didn't praise me as being better than them. We were all the same and treated the same. I don't know how to explain it. But down south, if a kid's skating around everyone, everyone starts talking about him. Up there, they knew I was good but there weren't any scouts watching us and it was no big deal.

When I was peewee age, I played with both the peewees and the bantams, but when I got a little older I just played with my brother and the other bantams. I wouldn't say I dominated at that level, but I definitely stood out. Every time we had a tournament, they'd say, "You've got to watch out for Tootoo." I just thought, being with my buddies, that we were all the same, and my buddies treated me like I was just the same. We all thought we were great players. For me, it wasn't like, *I'm the best player here so you've got to treat me differently.* It wasn't like that.

A few times each winter, we raised enough money to fly to other communities in the Keewatin region of Nunavut and we lit it up. Usually we won these tournaments. Rankin Inlet was the team to beat. But our community was a lot bigger than these other communities, so we also had a lot more kids.

THREE

Playing hockey in Rankin Inlet meant playing against the same kids Jordin had grown up with and then occasionally travelling to a neighbouring Inuit community such as Baker Lake or Chesterfield Inlet for a game. Rankin Inlet was a big city compared to those places, and their hockey teams didn't offer much of a challenge. But once a year, the Rankin Inlet players would head for more distant horizons. For Jordin, who knew that he was a very good player by local standards, it was a rare chance to experience a different part of the north and to put his skills to the test against kids who had enjoyed the benefit of playing in organized leagues.

In Rankin Inlet, we didn't have a hockey league. We just played with each other and we were always so rough and tough; our attitude was *anything goes*. Then, in March, we'd raise some money and the atoms and the peewees would go down to Yellowknife for a Native hockey tournament and just slaughter the other teams. They would be so scared of us. You could almost see them thinking, *Oh fuck, Rankin's coming and those guys are crazy.*

I remember that first time, jumping on a 737 and all of us, twelve- and thirteen-year-old kids, were thinking, *Holy shit, we're going to a huge city.* Yellowknife is like fucking Toronto or Vancouver to small-town kids. We'd never seen high-rises, so it was a big thing for us. And then we just dominated the tournament. We knew each other inside and out because we'd played together every day. Even nowadays, when guys from Rankin get together and play, they know where the other guys are going to be on the ice. You're playing with the same guys you grew up with, that you played with your whole life, right from when we were tykes. So you know everyone's moves.

In one of the games in Yellowknife, we were playing a team from Fort Providence, which is an Aboriginal community in the Northwest Territories about two hundred kilometres from Yellowknife. We were in peewees then, and I was just crushing guys. Guys were leaving the ice on stretchers. Everyone was raving about this fucking Tootoo kid, but they didn't believe I was only thirteen years old. There was a big scandal, and I had to prove my age.

But that's where I was spotted by the coach of the Fort Providence team, and it was the first time that anyone outside of Rankin Inlet had really noticed me as a hockey player. That summer, he called me at home and invited me to play for his team in the Alberta Native Provincial Hockey Championships in Edmonton.

I was ready to go and my parents gave their permission, but it was a little complicated. You had to be living in that community in order to play. So in January, when I was thirteen years old, I left for Fort Providence and moved in with a family just so I could play in this one tournament in June or July. It was a First Nations community but not Inuit. I didn't know a fucking soul. And life was different. They had trees in Fort Providence.

I was in grade eight then. For the rest of the school year I lived with the family there and went to class. Coming from a disrupted household already, I thought this was the greatest thing, because I wouldn't have to watch my parents party anymore. What a great opportunity this was to get out of my house and the fucking mess that it was behind closed doors. It was a big relief.

I KNOW I'VE TALKED about it already, but you really need to understand what my life was like at home then, what alcohol did to me and to my family.

For my parents, drinking starts out as a social thing, but then that social thing turns into fricking abuse and then into violence and that's when it takes control over them. They drink only to get fucking wasted.

Growing up, that was just normal for me. It's hard to get alcohol in Rankin and it's expensive. A lot of families are living paycheque to paycheque because of that; they set aside half of their paycheques to pay for their orders of booze.

There was booze in our house all the time. When I was ten, eleven, twelve years old, I'd open the cabinet under the sink and there'd be four or five bottles in there. *Fuck, I wonder what that tastes like.* But we kids were too scared to touch it because we knew if we did and got caught, we'd get the belt.

When my parents started drinking, Terence and I would take off. We always wanted to be outside then, away from the house, away from all of the bullshit. We'd be on our bikes riding to the Point, doing kid stuff, throwing rocks around, but it was always in our minds: *Fuck, if we do this, we're gonna get in shit.* If we got soakers in our boots, we'd stay away from home for as long as we could to try and dry up. We were two peas in a pod. We almost never left each other's side. And when we did, we'd ride around town looking for each other.

We had a lot of fun, and we were always finding different things to do. But we were always careful to never go over the edge, because if we did we would get the belt or the fucking wooden spoon when we got home. It's a small town. If Jordin and Terence Tootoo were breaking windows, our parents would find out. So we would watch our buddies do it, but we wouldn't do it—although even if we were around it, we'd be getting the boots from our parents.

We would come home and Mom would yell at us, or we'd get a fucking beating for some odd, stupid reason, or we'd be sent out to pick up Dad on the Ski-Doo when he was all pissed up and it was minus forty degrees. And we'd still have school the next day.

The truth is, my older sister, Corinne, was the one who put

up with the worst of the bullshit, the verbal and physical abuse at home, because she was the oldest and because she didn't have the chance to leave and play hockey the way Terence and I did. Drinking and abuse is a cycle for a lot of people in the north, and it's hard to break. If I didn't have hockey, I'd probably be a mechanic now, working for the town, living one day at a time, paycheque to paycheque. I'd probably have a bunch of kids running around. Leaving to go to Alberta for that tournament was huge for me.

When I do visits to other Inuit communities now, I talk about the importance of our culture and our traditions; you have to keep those strong. It all starts with the way our people carry themselves when they're out on the land. Nothing else matters other than living in the moment. You can't think beyond survival. You have one plan and that's to make sure you bring food back for your family. For a lot of our elders who grew up on the land, can you imagine how draining it must have been to go out into this wilderness where there are thousands and thousands of miles of open land and you need to find food? How are you going to do that? Where do you go? Our people have to be mentally tough.

When I visit the elders in our communities, they don't ask me about my hockey career. They ask how I am doing inside. It's not like they're proud of me because I'm an NHL star. That's when I know I am around our people—good people. Our elders know what it takes to survive. There are days when I want to throw in the towel and call it quits, but then I think of them and about what our people had to do back in the day just to stay alive. I'm an Inuk deep inside and I've got to make sure that I carry on those traditions.

The other thing I talk about is education. The dropout rate in the north is phenomenal. The teenagers are thinking, *Why do I need to go to school, because I'm never going anywhere anyway.* In a lot of the isolated communities I also try to get the kids to experience southern life, because it opens up more doors for them. But they're scared to leave. They all know about life in the south because of television, but they're scared of being put in a situation outside of their comfort zone and not knowing what to do when times get tough. They know what to do up here, but down there it's like a different language and, in a lot of ways, a different planet. That's why they stay. And then they get trapped.

SO I GOT AWAY from Rankin Inlet, got away from my folks, got away from all of the drinking and all of the bullshit. I moved in with my billet family in Fort Providence.

I walked into this new place and it was fine and dandy for the first week, fine for the second week, and then . . . well, frick, if I thought I was getting away from booze by moving south, I had another thing coming. It was awful, but it was all normal for me. I never complained about it because I still thought life in Fort Providence was better than it would have been at home. You learn to kind of hold everything in, and so I did that and just battled through it. At least I didn't have to worry about the belt or the wooden spoon like I would at home. So, no, I wasn't homesick.

They had three kids, including one the same age as me, and he was like a brother. Fuck, it wasn't healthy living, but to this day I still talk to those people. I guess I promised them that if I ever made it to the NHL, I was going to fly them down south so they could watch me play. They remind me of that when they come down to see me play in Edmonton or Calgary. I guess I never got around to it.

Outside of my billet house, I put my head down and just went about my business. But I was the new kid in school, and I ended up fighting kids all the time because I was picked on. I wasn't one of them. They tried to bully me. Well, I didn't take any shit from anyone. If you pissed me off, I'd beat the shit out of you. A month in, they knew better than to fuck with Jordin Tootoo.

It was a very hostile environment. But that's what I was used to, so it wasn't like I was shocked. There were a lot of drugs and alcohol. I tried marijuana there for the first time—it was a regular thing for a lot of these young kids because their parents did it all the time. But it just didn't do anything for me. Booze: that was my drug. First time I had it, I thought it was the greatest. I didn't care about weed. I never did hard drugs, cocaine or acid or whatever. It just never crossed my mind, because booze was always on my mind. I just thought it was natural because my parents did it and, well, fuck, if they did it, why couldn't I do it, too?

I played in the tournament in Edmonton and I ended up steamrolling a lot of the younger Aboriginal kids. I think that's when my name really started to get out there. They were saying,

"Who is this Tootoo kid? We've never seen anything like this before." I was just happy being away from home and having the opportunity to play in a big tournament.

Afterwards, a Triple A bantam coach pulled me aside and invited me to come to camp in Spruce Grove, which isn't far from Edmonton, and try out for his team. He sent the paperwork through to the coach in Fort Providence and I asked my parents about it. They said it was fine.

So that fall, at the beginning of grade nine, I moved to Spruce Grove, Alberta. My billets were another Aboriginal family—actually, there was another Aboriginal kid who had played in the tournament in Edmonton and then had moved to Spruce Grove to play for the same team. He lived with his single mother—just the two of them—and I moved in with them. It was a great situation. The mom was everything a kid coming down from the north could have asked for. She understood my whole background and situation. And it was a sober house. She didn't drink at all. That was all new to me—a good kind of new. Honestly, without her, I wouldn't be where I am today; I would have given everything up and said the hell with this. My other teammates' parents also welcomed me to their homes. Seeing how happy these families were . . . it was something I had never experienced before. It was awesome.

But the rest of my life in Spruce Grove wasn't so easy.

Needless to say, I made the team. Then, on my second shift in my first game of organized regular-season hockey, off the draw, a guy fucking slashed me. I thought, *Fuck you, white boy, don't fuck with me*, and I dropped my gloves. I ended up fighting a couple of guys, and all of the parents got wound up. After the game, I got a call telling me I was suspended for five games. I thought, *What the fuck is this? You guys want to play hockey? This isn't hockey.* Back home, if someone pissed you off, you just beat him up and then went back out and played. That's how I thought it was supposed to work, not with all of these fucking rules and systems and shit like that. In Rankin, it was just a free-for-all.

I served my time and word got around that Jordin Tootoo was fucking crazy. It was just my instincts. That's how I grew up. I was never the biggest guy out there, but I didn't take shit from anyone.

In school in Spruce Grove, there were only a handful of Aboriginal kids from the reserves around town, and a few East Indians, but of course I was the only Inuk. The white kids there thought they knew what the Native lifestyle was: fucking drunks and idiots and whatever. Obviously, I was put into that category right off the bat. I felt a bond with the Native kids. We're kind of the same people. We're cousins, even though we have different traditions and different beliefs. But I don't remember being particularly close to any of them at school.

What I do remember is the racism. A lot of racism. I wasn't used to that. I hadn't had a lot of experience with it. Growing up in our community, it always felt like everybody was equal. And when we'd go to tournaments in the surrounding communities, of course it was never an issue. The first time I really knew that racism even existed was when I was chosen to play for a Native all-star team at a tournament in Saskatoon when I was thirteen years old. The other teams got upset with us because we were playing the game the way we played it back home. We were rough and tough. We had come down south and it turned out that the rules were a lot different there. We were bulldozing everyone and they didn't like it—the players, the coaches, even the parents in the stands. On the ice, the kids started saying some pretty nasty stuff to us. You wonder how they came up with it. How did the adults teach these kids that it was okay to degrade someone of a different race? I can't recall many of the specific slurs now, but I remember being more surprised than hurt. A kid would yell something like, "Hey, Eskimo, go back and live in your igloo where you belong!" I remember thinking, *What's wrong with an igloo? What's wrong with being Inuit?* I just didn't get it.

But as I experienced more of those kinds of incidents over the years, I started to understand that I wasn't in Rankin anymore, where everyone knew everyone and everyone accepted everyone. I started to understand why a lot of people who left there came home soon after. I still hear stuff sometimes during a game. There was an incident during my rookie year in the NHL that got a bit of press. I got into a scrum with Tyler Wright in Columbus and he told the media afterwards that I bit his finger. Then he added, "Well, I guess that's what Eskimos do—they eat raw meat, don't they?" That was a racial slur.

I didn't hear about what Wright had said until it was in the papers and somebody contacted me to ask me what I thought. I told them that I didn't give a fuck what he'd said. I wasn't afraid of Wright, so I knew that one way or another he was going to get it. He was the type of player who was a chirper but who never really backed up his words. The next time we played Columbus, I knew something was going to happen—and he knew it, too. I already had the edge on him mentally. When he was getting ready in the dressing room that night, I know he was thinking, *Fuck, I've got to watch my back because Toots is going to do something stupid.* He was right. The game was in Nashville, and the whole crowd knew that something was going to happen. I went after Wright the minute we were both on the ice, and got three or four punches in. Then he turtled, as he usually did. It wasn't like any of his teammates were there to back him up. You're a man of your own words. If you say something, you'd better be there yourself to back it up.

That was the end of it. He never came around me again. He never said anything to me again. That was the end of that whole feud. And that's how a problem like that should be settled. In today's game, you've got all of these young punks roaming around the ice, saying shit and talking trash. As my father always says, "Talk is cheap, but money buys whisky." If you've got something to say, be a man. This doesn't apply just to hockey. In today's society, you see a lot of young kids being spoon-fed and having everything handed to them. When times are tough or they're faced with hardship, they'll just crumble.

OF COURSE, in Spruce Grove I was also the new kid on the block, this new hockey stud, which didn't help. I was built pretty much like I am now, maybe a little bit smaller.

Obviously, everyone's cliquey in high school. I had to really figure out who my friends were. And it turned out the only friends I had were my teammates. In class I would always hope that one of my teammates was there so I'd have someone to talk to. I wasn't the guy who would approach people or try to push myself to be cool like everyone else. I would always wait for them to welcome me in, and that would never happen. Except that some of the girls really liked me. They were saying, "Who is this cute little Jordin kid?" They were all over me. Of course, the guys said, "Fuck this guy. Who does he think he is, trying to take our girls away from us?" I remember getting into fights, standing up for myself.

The skater kids and the other cliques had their own little groups. I was an easy guy to pick on. I remember that guys would try to get into my locker, to burn my books and stuff. That happened. At first, I just took all of the heat. But then I stopped taking any more shit. I started calling guys out, guys who were trying to bully me. It got to the point where I lost it a couple of times. I remember walking home from school one day and hearing somebody behind me shouting, "Hey, fuck you!" I turned around and there were three kids walking up to me. I dropped my bag, started swinging for the fences, and beat the shit out of all three of them. I think, after that, no one really fucked with me. The message got out that it wasn't a good idea to fuck around with Tootoo. Don't even look at him, because he'll fucking kill you.

But still I kept hearing that so-called gangs from other schools were out to get me. Even when I walked down to the gas station, I was always looking over my shoulder. I thought that one of these gang kids was going to come after me.

I admit that I had a short fuse. With all of that anger inside me, I had no remorse when it came to hurting someone. And so I became the bully. I used that to my advantage, being the man in junior high. No one fucked around with me. When I left home, I assumed that if anyone pissed you off, that's what you did. Drop 'em. I was fighting in school. I got sent to the principal's office every now and then. And then I'd put the blame on the other person because, in my mind, I was just sticking up for myself.

It wasn't until midway through the school year that people started respecting me, because they knew what I could do on the ice. And I started arm wrestling these fucking tough guys in junior high, and I started killing them. Word started getting around. That's when I started gaining respect.

While I was in Spruce Grove, my only communication with Terence was through a fax machine. He was living in The Pas, playing for the OCN Blizzard (OCN stands for Opaskwayak Cree Nation). The band owns the team, which plays in the Manitoba Junior Hockey League, the level just below major junior. The OCN team started in 1996, and Terence started with them in 1997 and played for four seasons. The last three seasons, they won the league title, and the last two seasons, he was the team captain and the leading scorer.

A reporter from Toronto did a story on the Blizzard during Terence's last season there. He interviewed Terence about how hockey could be his ticket out of Rankin Inlet: "I have no respect for those kids who just give up," Terence said. "I see those guys when I go home for the summer and they're doing nothing. If you give up, you'll be a nobody." That was Terence.

Long-distance calls were expensive and the family I was living with in Spruce Grove couldn't afford it. So we communicated by writing pages and pages of faxes to each other, every day. We were constantly going to Staples to get more paper. Every day, I came home from school or from practice and it was straight to the machine, hoping that Terence had sent me a fax. I'd fax him to say, "I fucking hate it here. This sucks." And he'd say, "Jordin, just stick it out. This is going to be okay." He was always encouraging me to stay strong.

I wish I would have saved some of those faxes.

DURING THE YEAR that Terence was playing in The Pas and I was playing in Spruce Grove, his coaches started asking him about me. They caught wind that I was playing Triple A, and then they heard that I was taken by the Brandon Wheat Kings of the Western Hockey League in the bantam draft. Looking back, that was a big step for me—being drafted by a team in one of the best junior leagues in the world, where all kinds of NHL players had started their careers. As a fifteen-year-old, I was invited to the Wheat Kings' rookie camp, but there wasn't much chance I'd stick with the team that year. Instead, my plan was to go to Thompson, Manitoba, and play Midget AAA there. Thompson was only a two-hour drive from The Pas and a lot closer to home, so I'd have an easier time keeping in touch with Terence there.

The day after I got cut by the Wheat Kings, my dad and my brother drove down from The Pas to Brandon to pick me up and take me to Thompson. They came by at five o'clock in the morning and we started out on the first leg of the trip, the six-hour drive to The Pas. Instead of going straight on from there, we ended up staying overnight and checking out the beginning of OCN's training camp the next day. Terence was going to be in camp for a couple of days before I had to report to Thompson. The OCN coach, Gardiner MacDougall, asked Terence if I'd like to take a shot at making the team, and he told them I'd love to. So I suited up for a couple of exhibition games. Lit it up. Got in a few tilts. The next thing you know, the coaches were saying, "We want to keep you here." It happened so fast. Before I knew it, I was enrolled in the local high school and playing for OCN.

In hockey terms, it was a big jump. If I had gone to Thompson to play Midget, I would have been playing against fifteen- and sixteen-year olds. The OCN team played in a league that was just one level below major junior. The players there were all older: nineteen, twenty, and twenty-one. It was a really tight group. They were brought in from Ontario and Saskatchewan, as well as being from Manitoba. Only five or six of us were Aboriginal. These were guys who weren't going to play in the Canadian Hockey League, but they could come up to The Pas and play for good money, better money than they would make in major junior. I was fifteen years old and making five hundred bucks a week, with all of my living expenses covered.

Terence was making around $1200 a week because he was one of the top guys. And as a bonus, we could buy stuff on the reserve, like gas, tax-free.

As a hockey team, we were stacked. I think we lost only seven or eight games out of sixty-two that whole year. Gardiner MacDougall gave me an unbelievable opportunity to grow as a young player. At fifteen years old, I was playing with what were men to me and holding my own. That whole season, we were on fire. Our team was unbelievable. Visiting teams hated coming there because they knew they would get their asses kicked.

You could fit eight or nine hundred people in our home arena. I can just imagine teams crossing the bridge from The Pas to the reserve and seeing the arena there. They must have been shaking in their boots. It must have been a bad feeling knowing that they were going to get the shit kicked out of them in front of that hostile crowd.

We were living the life. I was one of the few guys still in school, so I'd go in the morning for two or three hours. Practice was at 12:30. We were done at 2:30. We'd show up for practice on snowmobiles and then everyone would go fishing after we were done—jump on the quads and go up the river to our ice shacks and just fish all afternoon. And we were getting paid to do it! That was probably the most fun I ever had as a hockey player. What more could a fifteen-year-old ask for? And I wasn't even supposed to be there. It just kind of happened.

Terence and I moved in together with a couple, Rosie and Ed, who were our billet family. Rosie was a schoolteacher and Ed worked at the pulp mill. As a fifteen- or sixteen-year-old kid, moving in with a billet family is one of the most intimidating things you can do. You grew up living with mom and dad all your life, and now you have to go and live with a family that has a different structure and different rules. Every billet family is different. Some of them are warm and loving, and some of them are just in it for the money they get from the team to house and feed you. As a player, you want to try to fit in and make sure you get off on the right foot. If things don't go well with a billet, that can be a determining factor in whether a kid wants to quit hockey or stick with it. Ideally, you want to make sure you have an environment where the family can cater to your needs and welcome you with open arms.

That's the way it was with Rosie and Ed. They were in their late fifties, early sixties, and they had grown-up kids who had moved out of the house. We were just something to keep them busy, and they liked having us around. It was a very healthy family, and they really looked out for me and my brother.

And OCN is also where I really started pumping the booze. Every weekend was a gong show for us. I was hanging out with older guys, and when you're part of the team, you're part of the team—it doesn't matter how old you are. I was in grade ten, but I was out in the bars with all of the boys. And the women. . . . We were fucking stud muffins, juggling different broads and telling stories and whatnot.

On those nights out, Terence looked after me. We liked to drink together, but I had to go to school in the morning. Some nights I would say, "Fuck it, let's get another case and keep going." And he'd be like a parent, and say, "Get to bed, you have to be ready for school tomorrow." I always knew I was in good hands.

We won a championship that season, and I was named OCN's scholastic player of the year. The truth is, because almost our whole team was nineteen or twenty years old, there were only two or three guys who were even in school. But I owe a lot to our billet Rosie, who took my education seriously because she was a teacher. I'd never really had someone hounding me to make sure I got my work done, on my ass every day, waking me up every morning, telling me it was time to go to school. And I'll tell you this: I had no fricking interest in going to school every day. I'd much rather have been living the life like all of the other nineteen-year-olds on my team. So kudos to Rosie. As much as I hated it then, it all worked out in the end.

But the best part of that year was being away from Rankin Inlet and being with Terence. Whatever was going on back home, we would back each other up. Every conversation we had with our parents, we made sure we'd find a way to let them know that everything was good at our end. No one had to tell us that things weren't so good at home. Terence would send a lot of his hockey money to our parents, just to please everyone and shut them up and keep them out of our hair. During his last two seasons there, after I left, he even took a side job at an auto body shop owned by the family he billeted with—Murray and Karen Haukass and their three boys, Brett, Luc, and Ty. Terence had always loved cars and he earned a little extra cash that way.

My brother's treat for me was that, after every practice, we would go through the Tim Hortons drive-through and he would buy me a French vanilla cappuccino and a doughnut. Always the same thing, and he always paid for it. It's one of those little things I miss. When I go to Tim Hortons now, I always have the same thing. There are times when I'm sitting in my car waiting for the order and I'm about to say something to Terence—but there's no one sitting next to me.

Through all those years, I thought that maybe we would wind up on the same team again somewhere down the road, maybe even in the NHL. But that was the last time we ever played together.

FOUR

The Western Hockey League—known in hockey circles as "The Dub"—is the youngest of Canada's three major junior hockey leagues, and once upon a time it was considered a poor prairie cousin of the established loops in Ontario and Quebec. But for decades now, the WHL has more than held its own, growing to include teams in the northwestern United States and becoming arguably the primary breeding ground for National Hockey League talent, especially the kind of big, bruising players who dominate the modern game. Growing up in Rankin Inlet, Jordin didn't have any direct exposure to The Dub until he was eleven years old, when family circumstances provided an unexpected look into his future.

In 1993, my dad went to school in Medicine Hat, Alberta, to get his plumber's trade certificate. We lived in a motel there for six months. It was just me and my mom and my dad. I did school work by correspondence and we all lived in a room the size of a living room. All I knew about the town was our motel, the street out front, and the rink where my dad played pick-up hockey with a couple of his buddies from plumbing school.

It turned out that was the same rink where the Medicine Hat Tigers played. One of his buddies saw me there with him and asked my dad if I played hockey, and he told him I did. Then, three months into our stay, a house league team asked me to come out. I was like, *Fuck, yeah!* I played a couple of games and I just lit it up. I wheeled around everyone and they were all saying, "Who is this kid?"

I remember going to watch the Tigers and thinking, *Holy fuck, it would be awesome to play in a rink like this.* It was the closest thing I had ever seen to the NHL.

One of the first things I did when I got the call from Kelly McCrimmon, telling me that I'd been drafted by the Brandon Wheat Kings, was to look up the team and see if they played in the same league as Medicine Hat. I remember thinking that I could be playing in that same league I saw as a kid if things worked out.

Kelly was the general manager and part-owner of the Wheat Kings. That's the way it works sometimes in junior hockey. He played junior hockey and college hockey, but he never played pro. His brother, though, was Brad McCrimmon, who played in the NHL and who was coaching in the Kontinental Hockey League in Russia when he was killed in that terrible plane crash in 2011.

When I was playing for OCN in that first season after I was drafted by the Wheat Kings and then cut in training camp, Kelly would come out to watch me whenever we came south to play games in Dauphin. The next year, I knew I had a good chance to make the Wheat Kings, which I did.

It was supposed to be a big step up from the Manitoba junior league to the WHL. I'll never forget the day I got my first paycheque. Remember, in The Pas I was making five hundred dollars a week, in cash. I figured that the WHL is a way bigger league, so you must get paid more. So when I signed my contract, I was gung-ho. Then payday came. I got a cheque for $72—and that was for two weeks. I called Terence and told him I was coming back to OCN. It was brutal. But then Kelly had me call my agent and he convinced me to stay in Brandon.

During that first season in Brandon, one of my best memories is of when I played my first game in Medicine Hat. I was skating around the rink before the game and just thinking, *Fuck, I'm back here. I can't believe this.* I remember the seats were like Smarties: all different colours. This is where I had been when I was a kid.

When I was leaving after the game, I saw a bunch of kids standing off to the side—fifteen or sixteen years old, so the same age as I was then. A girl came up to me and said, "Jordin, do you remember me?" I didn't know who she was. "I'm Kristen," she said. "I played hockey with you here in Medicine Hat and these are all the other guys you played with." Then I remembered— we had one girl on that house league team. And now here they all were. They remembered me. I thought that was pretty cool.

OFF THE ICE, my first two years in Brandon were really tough, in part because of the people I lived with. I was assigned to a billet family, which is the way it works in junior hockey. They are paid by the team to provide room and board. They had two kids who were younger than me, so their focus was on their kids and billeting me was just another income for them. At dinner or lunch, there was only enough food for them. And there was never any extra food around the house. I ended up going to my teammates' places to hang out because at least I knew there was food there.

So, I was miserable. Everything about the situation was killing me inside. Terence was still playing with OCN in The Pas, and when he'd come down to play in Dauphin, I'd just fuck off and go watch him because I wanted to be out of that house.

In August, after my second season in Brandon, Terence came down to visit me at the house. Everyone in the family was out. There was this other billet family I knew about—the couple's names were Neil and Jeanine. They were great people. Neil owned a golf course and a printing company, so they weren't housing players for the money. Neil was a real hoot to be around, the life of the party. He was a family guy who enjoyed life. And Jeanine was a passionate mother who always made sure there was food on the table. Her own boys came first, but she treated her billet players like they were part of the family. They'd had a twenty-year-old player living with them the season before, so he was going to be gone because he was overage. I knew that when the new season began, the Wheat Kings would send them another player.

So I grabbed six garbage bags and I said to Terence, "Help me pack up, I'm out of here." He said, "What are you doing?" I told him I was bringing my stuff to Neil and Jeanine's. We were going home to Rankin Inlet for a couple of weeks, and I figured I would just leave my stuff with them and stake my claim. So we packed up everything and I called Neil and Jeanine and asked them if I could store my stuff there until I got back. They said, "Okay, but aren't you living at Nigel and Kim's house?" I told them I wasn't happy there and that I was going to tell Kelly when I got back. Of course, Kelly caught wind of it before that and said, "No way you're going to move where you want to go."

By this time I was a star with the team, and I wasn't afraid of using my status to my advantage. So when I returned to Brandon I didn't even call my old billets. I had no contact with them. I was done. Instead, I walked into Neil and Jeanine's house and they said, "You need to call Kelly right now." I got on the phone with him and he blasted me: "Who the fuck do you think you are?" I told him that I didn't like it over there. I told him: "This is where I want to live; I'm going to live here. End of story." I know now how immature and selfish that was, but I didn't care about anyone else. I was telling the general manager what I was doing—as a kid—and who does that?

But in the end I got my way and ended up staying with Neil and Jeanine, and life was great. I ended up there for the last two years of junior. Their place was out in the country a little bit and they had two boys who were a little younger than me, and everything just clicked perfectly. I was a lot happier, and they were a stable family. Slowly I started opening up to them. They had a better understanding of me and the shit I'd been through. It was like a weight lifted off my shoulders. They actually cared about me. I realized they would go to war for me. I felt loved. I felt part of a family again. I have to thank them for giving me the opportunity to open up and be myself.

THERE WAS ANOTHER THING I liked about my new billets: they loved having parties. Sometimes we'd have team parties at their place, so I figured it would be the perfect spot for me, because by then partying had become a big part of my life.

I was fourteen when I first tried alcohol. It was just us kids drinking out behind a building in Rankin Inlet. I'd be watching my parents drink: it's a Friday night, Dad's getting off work, and it's building up. So I'd steal a couple of shots just to warm up the blood a bit. Then in The Pas, when I was playing for OCN, I hung out with Terence and the older guys and could do pretty much whatever I wanted, which included a lot of drinking.

When I got to Brandon, for the first two years I was still in high school, so I was a bit controlled and life at a billet home is structured. But even then, every once in a while I would get fucking blasted. At the beginning I was really shy, except when we had team parties. Then I would light 'er up and stories would start getting out. But all of those stories would go away after I scored a hat trick.

Then during the last two years of junior, because I was out of school, an older guy, and a top player, I figured I could get away with a lot. Which I did.

The way people drink back home influenced my drinking when I went down south. It was always drink until you're drunk, drink your sorrows away so you don't fucking have any pain and you don't remember anything and you just forget about everything. Up in Rankin, you drink until the last drop's gone, and then you find someone else with booze. You figure out the consequences later. That's the way I was.

Not that anyone in Brandon would have understood that. They thought I was the life of the party. I was on top of the world. I was playing junior hockey in a place where it was the biggest game in town, I was the best player on my team, the leading scorer, and drinking was already second nature to me. I figured that no one was ever going to give me shit about what I did off the ice, and if they did I'd fucking prove them wrong. That's what I've been doing all my life.

In Brandon I could always find friends to party with, and I always thought I could handle my booze. I was a guy who drank a lot, but I wasn't a guy who would start fighting when I drank. I was a happy drunk. I had seen all the negativity and anger in my family when they started drinking, and I didn't fucking want to be like that.

I felt invincible; I was scoring goals and leading my team and the fans loved me. The fans didn't know anything about my other life; they didn't know that I partied hard. Only my teammates and friends knew. My parents didn't know—if they had, they'd have fricking killed me. They would have told me that I was disgracing our family name and shit like that.

I knew that when push came to shove, hockey made up

for anything I did in my personal life. I was fucking dominant on the ice. If I stayed dominant, the people running the team didn't care about anything else, because ultimately you're there for hockey. So I was living two lives. And as for my billets, it was like this: I'd bring a case of beer home and they'd say, "What are you doing?"

I'd tell them that I was going to sit in the basement and have a few beers.

"No, you're not."

"Fuck you, I'm not. I am. Fucking don't tell me what to do." And that was that.

My standard routine was to pick up a twelve-pack and get half cut. If we had team parties it was like, "Toots is just going to get ripped tonight. Fucking A." And in the off-season, when my brother was around with our buddies, it was four- or five-day benders. Party all night, sleep all day, regroup, do it again, send home a couple grand to shut my parents up for the week, then back at it again. Life was good.

As a hockey player, I could get away with it. I knew I was good and that compensated for whatever else I did. If I went out partying and missed curfew—fuck it, I'm going to score two goals and three assists tonight, so that will block everything out. And that's exactly what happened. In juniors I would party hard and be fucking hung over, but I just battled through it during games because, growing up, I was mentally tough. I battled through a lot of shit because that was in my blood. Even when I turned pro, it was the same thing: play five or seven minutes in a game, get in a couple of fights, and it's all good.

I got called into the office by Kelly McCrimmon countless times. I had countless battles with him. It got to the point where it became one long fuck-you match. I remember one time specifically the Tragically Hip was in town to play on a Saturday night. Kelly scheduled a practice for eleven o'clock on Sunday morning because he didn't want the guys who were going to the concert to stay out all night. Of course, I went to the concert and ended up meeting a broad and didn't even go home. I slept through practice. Well, fuck, I woke up in this broad's house and it was 12:30. There were a bunch of missed calls on my phone from Kelly, and the assistant coach, and my agent. I went home to my billets and they were worried sick. They told me I needed to go see Kelly right away. I called my agent first and gave him the lowdown. And then I called Kelly and he lashed out at me, said I'd better get my ass down to the rink right away. So, of course, I was in panic mode—and not for the first time. I was shitting my pants. But when I got there, I sure didn't act that way.

Kelly pulled me into his office and started yelling: "What the fuck are you doing? We're going to send you home! This is not right! We're taking the A (for alternate captain) off of you! You're not a good leader!" He told me he was suspending me for a week for partying and missing practice. I said, right to his face, "You're sending me home? Then trade me right fucking now. I'm out of here; I'm done. You're not going to tell me what to do. I'm the man here. I'm the fucking leading scorer, and I've got a beautiful girl by my side." I was so pissed off I was going to fight three guys that night—fight, do my shit, get half cut, and it's all good. That was my attitude. And, of course, there was no way they were going to trade me. They needed me.

But, sure, that was a bit of a wake-up call for me. For a minute I thought, *Holy fuck, I can't be doing this.* But it didn't stop me. Because I knew at the end of the day that if I did my job on the ice and we won a few games, all would be forgiven.

A few hours later, Kelly called me to cool things off. But I was suspended for the week. I couldn't even go to the rink. People noticed that I wasn't around and that I missed a couple of games, but the real story never got out.

The truth is, I owe Kelly McCrimmon a lot. All of the stuff about my drinking stayed within the organization. It didn't even get out to my parents. If my parents had got wind of it, I knew I'd be in deep shit. I was always scared of my parents. And it didn't get out to the NHL scouts who were coming to look at me. I can't thank Kelly enough for that. If he weren't a truly genuine guy who cared about his players, I wouldn't even have been drafted. For some reason, he saw the good side of me.

WHILE I WAS PLAYING in Brandon, Terence would come down and stay with me after his season ended, and then we would go home to Rankin Inlet for a couple of weeks. And that was a whole other scene, back there putting up with the parents' drinking and listening to their sob stories about not having enough money. I don't think my parents ever understood how much partying I did, and I sure didn't tell them. The less

I told them, the better my life was, because they had their own shit to worry about. I'm their son, not their parent.

There were daily phone calls between me and Terence when he was in The Pas and I was in Brandon. "Did you call Mom? Dad?" "No, you call." Neither of us wanted to have to listen to their bullshit. We moved away from town to get away from that shit. But it was constantly with us, because we were always worrying about what was going on. Is Corinne okay? She had her own family by then and the next thing you knew, her kids were growing up around my parents; it was an unhealthy environment.

Not a lot of people know that I even have a sister. Corinne's one tough cookie. She had to be to put up with so much mental abuse and physical abuse. Her being as strong as she is today is unbelievable. When I was a young kid, it seemed like she was always in the doghouse with our parents. It was hard for me, as a younger brother, to see my sister be in shit all the time for no reason. When my parents were partying and drinking, they'd bring everything on Corinne. She did her fair share of drinking in her early teens as well, but ever since she had her first kid when she was twenty-one, I don't remember her drinking. Now she's got a happy, healthy family, a husband, and four kids. She's sober and her husband is sober.

When my brother and I left home, there was a void there for my parents. Then Corinne started having kids and that filled the void. When she started having kids, my parents kind of took over and started looking after them. Seeing my nephews and nieces having to deal with my parents' old-school mentality . . .

that's not how it's supposed to be anymore. But when I say stuff like that to Corinne, she laughs and says, "Imagine living here every day and seeing the shit that goes on—you wouldn't know what to do."

The truth is, Corinne is my best friend. I can call her any night of the week. She's the only one who has known me through thick and thin. We talk every other day, and I'm not afraid to talk to her about anything. We've always been close. She kind of took me under her wing when I was a little kid. We talk to each other when things aren't going well. She says, "You're my little brother. I can give you shit just like Mom does." She's someone I look up to a lot.

For her, having to deal with everyday life living in the north and with our family situation is tough. Sometimes she'll bitch about how it sucks up there and complain that this is all we've got. But she's not going anywhere. Terence and I got out, but Corinne always says that she's a lifer. She would never leave Rankin Inlet.

MONEY WAS ALWAYS a big issue for my parents, and it still is. Sure, it's expensive to live in the north. My parents both worked—my dad is retired now, but my mom still works as a school janitor. But it wasn't about buying gas or groceries. It was about the booze, and about the fact that they always expected things to be given to them because they figured they had made us.

I was making only a couple hundred bucks a week playing junior. Terence was making more than that in The Pas. But with both of us, half of that had to go home—and, fuck, we knew what it was being spent on. Mom would call and say, "We can't make our payments."

"You need fuel? You need food? What's the grocery store's number? I'll call the gas station and open a tab for you."

"No, just send us some money."

I knew what they were really trying to get at. They wanted to order booze.

Usually it wasn't my dad who asked for the money; it was Mom: "I got no money. Dad doesn't know how to pay bills. I got to pay everything." Well, meanwhile, my mom's playing bingo three times a week, plus buying booze. She always had an excuse, but in the end she was just using us. She used her kids to pay for her fucking addictions.

My parents still think I'm the Jordin who will just give, give, give, give, give, and nothing's ever good enough for them. You know, I called home and told them I bought a new truck, and their reaction was, "Why would you buy a sixty-thousand-dollar car when you could have spent that money elsewhere?" In their minds they're thinking, *There's sixty thousand gone and no money for us.* It's never: "Oh, I'm proud of you" or "Congratulations!" There's never any encouragement or anything. When I told them I bought my place in Kelowna, my mom gave me the old "Well, fuck, that's not very smart of you to spend two million dollars on a house and fucking waste all your money on that."

Like, what's wrong with you? Mom, I fucking worked hard all my life for this. Why can't you just say congratulations and leave it at that?

BACK THEN, coming home in the summer meant that I was partying right alongside my parents and everyone else. That's actually when I drank the most. It was my time off. People in the community would be amazed, seeing me and Terence drunk so often. They'd be thinking, *Holy shit, do they live like that all the time? When do they ever play hockey?* But no one complained— especially my parents—because we supplied the booze. They sure weren't going to tell their kids not to drink and at the same time drink the booze we were providing.

In Rankin Inlet, alcohol is supposed to be controlled, and you're supposed to need a permit to bring booze in. Not when I came home. It was a big piss-up. I'd bring up cases and cases of beer—coolers full of beer—plus the hard stuff, all brought home on the plane. Our bedroom was like a liquor store and, for our parents, it was like, *Fuck, yeah, this is fucking great.* They'd place an order before we came home—we need ten cases of this and five bottles of that—and we would deliver it. I would come home with ten checked bags with bottles clinking inside them and no one fucking questioned me.

Then it would be one long fucking shindig until we left again. The whole town would be fucking hammered thanks to us. The word would get out that Jordin and Terence were home and partying somewhere, so have at 'er. All our buddies and relatives would show up, and we'd all party together.

The whole time I was home it'd just be one drama after another—my buddies feuding with their girlfriends, and husbands fighting with wives, and older guys partying and getting thrown in the drunk tank—but I didn't fucking care. It was a circus, but I didn't care because we were having fun. A lot of my friends and people in the community don't drink that often, but when they do it's mayhem. Like I said, you turned into a fricking devil. Back then, I never understood why my buddies' girlfriends would get pissed off at them for partying with me. Well, now I know that when they'd go home and they were pissed drunk, it was a different story—and I didn't have to deal with it.

You don't see that when you're living in that cloud. But now, when I come home, I think, *What the fuck was I doing?* Being selfish, and doing it all for the wrong reasons. To us, bringing the booze home was a way to have fun and shut up our parents, but it caused so much shit for so many other people.

Jordin's first season with the Brandon Wheat Kings was 1999–2000. Playing as a sixteen-year-old, he scored only 6 goals in 45 games, but made a statement with his 217 penalty minutes. Though he was young, and far from the biggest guy on his team, he made it clear that he wouldn't back down from anyone. He was already on the radar of Hockey Canada, dating back to his minor hockey days in Alberta. The organization invited him to participate in a program designed to take the best young hockey players in Canada and groom them to compete for the country internationally, with the big prize being a spot on the World Junior Championship team. Thanks to blanket television coverage on TSN over the Christmas season, when fans were at home with few other sports viewing options, and thanks especially to regular Canadian victories, the World Juniors had become one of the most watched sporting events on the calendar. Canadians fell in love with international hockey while watching the legendary Summit Series in 1972, and each subsequent tournament was framed as a battle for the national birthright. The World Juniors fed on those emotions, each year delivering a new crop of fresh-faced heroes, wearing the maple leaf and battling against whichever country emerged as the great rival—the Russians, the Americans, the Swedes, or the Finns. Some of the players involved would go on to become stars in the National Hockey League, while for others the World Juniors would mark the peak of their celebrity, and sometimes the peak of their hockey careers.

Playing junior hockey in Brandon wasn't a big leap from OCN, because I had already spent a year playing against guys who were junior age. The only real difference was the travel—the long road trips in The Dub. We didn't have those in The Pas.

In my first year of junior, I got to play on two teams that were part of Hockey Canada's Program of Excellence, which identifies the best players in the country and prepares them for the World Juniors. First, I was part of Team West, which represented Manitoba and Saskatchewan in the World Under-17 Hockey Challenge, played in Timmins, Ontario. There were four other

Canadian teams representing different regions, plus teams from Germany, the Czech Republic, Russia, the United States, and Finland. That year, the Russians won the tournament.

Then, in the summer between my first and second years in Brandon, I was picked to play on the National Men's Under-18 Team in what was then called the Four Nations Tournament in Kežmarok, Slovakia. (It's now called the Ivan Hlinka Memorial Tournament.) The other three countries involved were Slovakia, the Czech Republic, and the United States. That was the first time I'd been outside North America and the first time I'd spent seven or eight hours flying anywhere. So, it was a whole new experience for me. As I remember, the food and the hotel were a little greasy, but I'd been in worse places and eaten worse things out on the land, so it wasn't that big of a deal for me.

There were some great players on that team: Derek Roy, Scottie Upshall, Stephen Weiss. A bunch of guys who went on to play in the NHL. With those kinds of tournaments, you have to come together pretty damn quickly and bond as a team. It helps if you can have fun and enjoy it. That was a great group of young guys. I remember before every game, after our warm-up stretches, we'd form a circle and everyone would take turns doing a little dance in the middle. I was a pretty shy guy. But when you're in that environment and everyone enjoys it, even if you're not a dancer you come up with something and everybody starts cheering.

Right before the tournament began, I was named captain, which was a huge honour, especially when you look at who was on that team. We ran the table, beating the Americans 3–1 in the final game to win the championship. That was pretty amazing: seeing the flag raised and hearing "O Canada."

When you put on that maple leaf and represent your country—fuck, you're on top of the world! You're sixteen, seventeen, eighteen years old and playing for Canada. What could be better than that? At that age you don't really feel how much pressure there is on you to win the gold medal. You just enjoy it. You just go out and play the game. After those two tournaments, I knew I had a chance to play on the World Juniors team. That would be a whole other level.

WHEN I FIRST MOVED to Brandon, and moved out of the billet house I'd shared with Terence in The Pas, Mike Young moved in with him and lived with the Haukass family. Mike ended up becoming one of my best friends. He has been through thick and thin with me. He probably got to know Terence as well as anyone. He looked up to Terence and wound up living with him for two years. To this day, Mike and I reminisce about all of the good times we had with him. When we go out fishing or hunting or just do random things together, Terence's name always comes up. I really appreciate having a best friend who knows what kind of a guy my brother was and who can relate to my experiences with him.

Mike comes from Gillam, Manitoba, way up in the northern part of the province. I think it really worked out well for him, moving in with my brother, because they were both from small towns, both from pretty isolated communities. Having a support system with one other person who could relate to where they'd come from worked out for both of them. Terence kind of took Mike under his wing in The Pas. Terence was one of the veteran guys at OCN and Mike is the same age as me—so, three years younger than Terence was.

Mike played for a couple of years in The Pas with Terence and then came to Brandon to try out with the Wheat Kings. He made the team and hung on for a few months, so we ended up playing together for a little while. After that, he went on to play pro in the Central Hockey League in the States, and now he lives in Dallas and runs the elite youth program for the Dallas Stars. He's gone into the coaching side of hockey, and good for him. There aren't a lot of guys who move south from Canada and stay down there.

I have to tell you a story about our time together in Brandon. One night, I was invited to a hot-tub party that was being thrown by a bunch of my girlfriends. I was a veteran on the team at that point and Mike was a rookie, so I had to egg him on a bit to get him to come out with me. He was worried, because we were supposed to have a ten o'clock curfew that night. We had a game in Saskatoon, which is a six-hour bus ride from Brandon, the next night and the bus was leaving at six o'clock the next morning. But I guess the combination of me encouraging him and the thought of those girls in the hot tub persuaded him that it was a good idea.

We grabbed a case of beer and headed over to the party around 8:30. The minute we got there, we jumped into the hot tub with a bunch of ladies, and that was good—me and Mike and five or six girls. Forty minutes went by and our case of beer was gone. *Well, why don't we wind 'er up and grab another case?* So we went out and grabbed another case of beer, and by that time it was right around ten o'clock—right around our curfew—but we didn't care. So, that second case of beer fricking got us drunk. *Well, boys, let's grab another case of beer.* So, by then we were a few cases deep and three sheets to the wind and the next thing we knew it was one o'clock in the morning. The bus was leaving at six o'clock. So, what the hell were we going to do? Thank God I had an extra suit in the back of my car from a previous road trip; we always had to wear a suit and tie when we went on a road trip.

I ended up crashing at Mike's billet house with him. I remember, just before passing out, that Mike said, "Toots, whatever you do, make sure you set two alarms on your phone. I'm setting my house alarm and my phone to make sure we wake up on time." *Yeah, yeah, no worries, no worries.*

Lo and behold, we slept through our alarms and it was 6:15 when we woke up. You can imagine our panic. We were still half-drunk and losing it, scrambling around and gathering our shit together, trying to get out the door. We showed up at the rink around 6:30 and the bus was waiting outside with everybody already on it. I stormed into the arena to pack up my gear and I remember that our trainer grabbed me and said, "Toots, don't worry, we packed your bag already. Get the hell on the bus." So, I cruised onto the bus trying to look like everything was fine, with my scarf wrapped around my face because I knew that I definitely reeked of booze. I went right to the back of the bus and took my usual position for long road trips: crashing out on the floor. I looked up and saw Mike moseying his way onto the bus. Of course, because he was a rookie, he had to sit right up front where the coaches sat. He was covering his face as best he could. Once we got moving, I fell asleep pretty fast, but I remember one of my teammates waking me up and saying, "Holy shit, Toots, you smell like a brewery." After that, I passed out and went into a deep, deep sleep.

Around Regina, which is about four hours outside Brandon, the bus got stuck in the snow. Everyone had to get off, but I was so out of it that the guys figured they might as well just let me sleep there. I didn't even know it had happened until we got to Saskatoon and they told me about it. That was right near the end of Mike's stint in the WHL. He was a bubble guy and we had a couple of young prospects who the team decided to go with instead of him. He ended up going back to OCN and playing out the rest of his junior career there.

Oh yeah, and when we played the Blades in Saskatoon that night, I scored 2 goals, got a couple of assists, and was named the first star of the game.

FIVE

*A*t the end of the 2000–2001 season, just before heading
overseas for the tournament in Slovakia, Jordin returned
home to Rankin Inlet to visit his family. It was becoming more and
more obvious that someday he might have a chance to do what no
Inuk had done before: play in the National Hockey League. Being
a junior hockey star was one thing, but making it to the NHL,
to the big time, would open the door to an entirely different level
of fame . . . and wealth. But when Jordin arrived home for his
annual summer return to the north, knowing that his own life
was about to change dramatically, he realized immediately what
would always stay the same. In the claustrophobic confines of the
Tootoo home, the cycle of drinking, abuse, and occasional violence
continued as it had for most of his life. Jordin's father, Barney, was
still two different people: the person he was when he was sober,
and especially when he was out on the land, and the person he was
when he was drinking. Everyone in the family lived in fear of the

next binge. From an early age, Jordin's and Terence's role had been to try to manage their parents, to defuse the anger, to pick up the pieces, all while pretending to the outside world that everything was fine in the Tootoo home. They learned to lie, to cover up, and to survive. That was the way it had been since they were children, walking the streets to find Barney and get him home safely after one of his benders, when they were trying to protect their sister, Corinne, when they were breaking up fights between their parents or following their mother when she fled town temporarily to get away from their father. Even though they had grown into young men, their roles hadn't really evolved. And then one day came a breaking point, when the balance of power shifted forever. Barney was drunk again. Jordin knew that script by heart. He knew how it had always ended. But this time, it would be different.

My father is highly respected in our community. He isn't the biggest guy, but no one fucks with Barney Tootoo. Everyone looks up to him. In Rankin Inlet, they think of him as a great guy. When I was growing up, all of my buddies considered him a mentor. I think that in a lot of small communities you've got the "chief" who everyone follows. That's my dad. And he thinks he can do whatever he wants, whenever he wants, because everyone respects him. But when my father drinks, especially hard liquor, he becomes an evil monster, a fucking scary guy. Everyone is intimidated by him.

His parents were alcoholics. It's cyclical. It's just what you grew up with. His parents drank, he drank, and Terence and I drank. I don't ever want my kids to have to deal with that and it's one of the biggest reasons why I called it quits and changed my life. My sister, Corinne, is sober. As a young teenager, she was a bit rebellious and did some drinking, but by the time I started drinking she had quit. I never saw her out partying, because she was already fed up with it. When I was partying, I'd always try to get her to drink, but she wouldn't do it. I'd wonder what the fuck was wrong with her, because I was messed up myself. I was caught up in all of that bullshit.

My dad is mostly a weekend binge drinker. Booze is $150 for a forty-ouncer or a case of beer up north. Most people didn't drink beer because it took up too much room and you needed more of it to get drunk, so liquor was easier to access. Our family had connections in Churchill, where my grandmother lived. It was no sweat to get booze there, because you could just go to a provincial liquor store and buy it. And then you just had to get it on the plane. My grandma lived in Churchill, so you know it was an easy supply line.

In a small town, you don't want to show people weakness, but behind closed doors it's a different story. I remember when I was a kid and it would be Friday. Dad came home at five o'clock. You knew it was going to be a long weekend when he brought out the bottle at fucking 5:10. Once the bottle came out, you knew shit was going to go down, and it wasn't going to be fun. We kids would go into hiding, because you never knew what was going to happen. A couple of hours later, he was going to be tanked and it was going to be a fucking disaster. As for my mom, she was thinking, *Well, I might as well grab a drink to keep myself on the same level.*

We'd say to ourselves, "Aw, Dad's drinking again," and go out to play street hockey just to get away from that environment. At 8:30 or 9:00 they'd be fucking yelling out the window: "Get your ass inside the house!" You knew it wasn't going to be a good Friday, Saturday, or Sunday when you heard that. My friends didn't know anything about it, and I didn't know if it was going on in their homes, too.

My parents were strict, but when they were half cut they were mean, and it wasn't fun when you had to come home and listen to them arguing and scuffling. I remember jumping on a plane one Friday night, fucking off and going to Churchill because my mom had had enough of the harassment and shit from my dad. We jumped on a plane, the three kids and my mom, just to get away.

But usually we would sit in our bedroom crying, and then you'd hear them scream our fucking names: "Come down here and make me something to eat!" I spent a lot of time being looked after by my sister and my brother. They took a lot of the heat. I would do something in the house that would piss off our parents and my sister and brother would take the heat for it. I was just a kid. I didn't know better.

Even my close buddies who I grew up with didn't like drinking with my dad. He would complain that no one ever wanted to come around and have a few beers with him. Well, duh. . . . You're an animal. Who wants to drink with someone who gets so negative and also thinks he's king shit?

Even the RCMP in Rankin Inlet knew better than to fuck with my dad, except for one guy. Dad was walking home piss-drunk one night and a cop picked him up. Dad said, "Who the fuck are you? How dare you do this to me?" The cop arrested him and threw him in the drunk tank. The cop was a new guy. He didn't understand. He didn't know who Barney Tootoo was. A week later, that cop was gone.

THE LAST TIME my dad hit the bottle was during the summer I beat him up. That's when he was still on the hard stuff. We were all partying at the house. When you drink, there's that fine line where if you cross it, you know you're going to snap. He was drunk, I was drunk, he said something, and I fucking snapped.

No one had ever heard those words from him before, and they really set me off: "You're not my fucking son. I'm not your fucking dad, so fuck you." When he told me that, it just made me go fucking crazy and I grabbed him and started beating him. My sister and my mom were right there trying to stop me. My mom was freaking out, fucking going apeshit.

"I'm not your father." I don't think he really meant that I wasn't his biological son. I think it was something less than that. When you're at that stage of intoxication, your brain isn't functioning well. I'm pretty sure him saying that was a spontaneous thing, but to this day I really don't know.

What I do know is that it was the moment in my life when I was finally fed up with all of the fucking bullshit. Before that, I had taken it. We had all taken it. And Terence was too scared to fight back, because my dad had control of him. Terence knew that if he pissed Dad off, Dad was going to fucking give it to him. My brother was like his right-hand man. Because he was the older boy, when Dad needed a hunting partner, Terence was there. When he needed a babysitter, my brother was there. He had Terence under his thumb. And all of that just fucking piled up in Terence's brain.

For me, it was different. And on that day, it was as if all the anger and frustration that had been building up for my whole life had to be let out. I'd had enough. I'd had enough of watching my dad be that monster to my family, to my mom and my sister. After all of those years of getting abused, I finally said fuck it. I was just sick of all of it. It was time to fucking step up. "You want to fuck around? Let's go. I'm a man now. There's no more of this. You're not going to fucking push me around anymore and treat me like an inmate." I got up and started a fucking shoving match with him right in front of my mom and my sister. The doors were all closed and shit was flying everywhere in the house and then I just fucking laid into him. I let it all out, all of that anger, and beat the hell out of him. That was me saying, *Fuck you, Dad. You're telling me I'm not your son? I'll fucking show you.*

Afterwards, I was in shock. I hadn't realized how strong I was. My dad hadn't realized that either. He thought I was still a little kid that he could push around. But, no more. I beat him up good. He was wearing a T-shirt and by the end of the fight it was ripped to shreds and covered with blood. When it was over, I picked the shirt up off the floor and handed it to my sister. "Here you go, Corinne. Keep that as a souvenir." I don't know if she still has it. It's never been brought up again, but I'll have to ask her to pull it out one of these days. Maybe she has it framed.

It was all over within thirty minutes. And that was a turning point. It felt like shit lifted off of my shoulders. It got all the anger and frustration out of me and onto him. Afterwards, my mother gave me shit for doing it. She said, "Why would you do that to your father? What's wrong with you?" I thought, *Fuck you, too. You guys raised me on a leash. I could only be in certain areas of the house and I could only say certain things. Now I'm a grown-ass man. I'm not a fucking kid who you can toss around and bitch-slap and force to look after you. I'm fucking playing junior hockey and making peanuts and you're calling me and asking me for money, telling me, "You'd better send me money or you're going to get it when you come home." No more. Fuck you.*

After the fight, I walked out of the house like nothing had happened. I left everything there, went to my sister's house, and shed a few tears with her. I stayed there for a few days. After that, nobody knew what had happened, not even my best friends. When they asked why I was all scraped up, I just made up a lie.

"Where's your dad? We haven't seen him in a couple of days."

"Aw, he's sick, you know."

In my family, we knew how to weasel our way around those kinds of questions.

My father retreated to my parents' bedroom. I'm sure he was black and blue, but I didn't see him for a whole week. I wasn't going home. I wasn't going to fucking talk to him after him telling me he's not my dad. A day went by and there was no sign of him. Two days, three days: still nothing. I wasn't going

75

to approach him. I was waiting for him to apologize for all that he'd done. My mom asked me if I was going to talk to him. I said, "Fuck, no, I'm not talking to him." She said, "He's asking me questions about what happened." He had blacked out. My dad acted like he didn't remember a thing. That's the way he is. I told her she could tell him what had happened, because I wasn't going to do it.

Finally, my mom told him straight out what had happened and then, about a week after the fight, he approached me and told me he was sorry for his actions. And I was just like, *Okay, whatever.* But I was still fucking furious. A guy you grew up with all of your life, who you called Dad, all of a sudden tells you he's not your dad and you're not his son. . . . A week after that, I took off back down south. I had to go back to Brandon. Nobody outside the family knew what had happened.

Terence had been in The Pas when I fought Dad. I told him about it when I returned down south. How could you not tell your best friend something like that? His initial reaction was to wonder whether he was somehow going to wind up taking the heat for it. But then he gave me a look that said, *Fuck, yeah.* He didn't want to show that he was happy about it, but I think he felt that inside of him. He was so tight with our dad that I don't think he would have ever gotten to that point with him. But he understood why I did it.

Relations with the family were pretty hostile for a long time after that. I didn't want to go home in the next off-season, so Terence and I spent half of the summer in The Pas and then went to Brandon. We lied our way through everything with our parents, saying we had to do hockey schools or were trying to earn extra cash. We knew how to lie because we were brought up lying. Meanwhile, we were partying and didn't have to put up with their antics.

When I finally did go back home the next summer, it was like nothing had happened. It was back to partying. The only difference was that Dad knew he couldn't control the liquor, so he'd switched to beer. That fight changed our relationship. It was a stepping stone. It was a way of letting him know I wasn't a kid anymore, that I was going to start standing up for myself. He knew, now. He knew what would happen if he ever pissed me off like that again. And he never did.

SIX

The following season, his second in junior hockey, would be a significant one for Jordin. Because he turned eighteen on February 2, he was eligible for the National Hockey League draft. No one of Inuit descent had ever played in the league before. By now, anyone who watched the Wheat Kings knew that Jordin was tough and that he was willing to drop the gloves when called upon. He easily could have been pigeonholed in the enforcer's role. But there was more to his game than fighting: the speed and skills and scoring touch that would soon make him a first-line player in major junior hockey. Kelly McCrimmon, the coach and general manager of the Wheat Kings, was the first to understand Jordin's potential and to give him the chance to become a complete player.

The fact is, if it weren't for Kelly McCrimmon, I wouldn't be where I am today. He was the one person who believed in me and gave me every opportunity to grow as a hockey player. I think he saw something in me that no other person in the hockey world did. Plus, he's a person who cares a lot for his players. He's played hockey himself, so he understands how players feel and how they think.

It's not like we always got along. We had many disagreements and battles, as you've already heard. But that was part of me being a young, egotistical hockey player who thinks he has everyone by the balls and can do anything he wants. Kelly definitely put me in my place many times and I thank him for doing that. There were some dark times when I could have just given up and said, *The hell with it, I'm out of here.* But he kept hounding me in all the right ways.

Kelly sensed that I had more in me as a hockey player, and I seized that opportunity. He must just have a knack for knowing, for picking out certain players. He definitely sensed that with me. Kelly knew what type of player I was and that I meant a lot to the team, but he's also the one who saw my offensive skills. I was more of a guy who thought he could just be a physical presence and not worry about scoring goals and putting up points. Kelly brought me into his office many times and said, "Hey, everybody in the league knows you're tough. There's a time and place for fighting and being physical. But you can score in this league. You have a great shot. You're one of the fastest guys in the league. We need you to focus more on that."

I didn't know I had that in me. But when a coach believes in you and trusts you and gives you an opportunity, you can break through those limitations. In my draft year I was just starting to figure that out, but obviously some of the scouts—who also must have been talking to Kelly—were starting to see that potential.

Early in 2001, Kelly called me into his office and told me I had been selected to play in the CHL Top Prospects Game. Apparently, that meant I was considered one of the forty top draft-eligible players in Canadian junior hockey. But at that age I didn't really understand how the hockey world worked regarding the draft and rankings and all that. For me, the important thing was that it was kind of cool. *I'm going to play with other great players in Calgary? That's great. Awesome.* I didn't realize the significance it could have in my draft year. I just got on the plane and enjoyed myself, and enjoyed all of the great hockey players I was surrounded by—guys who are in the NHL now. It was an honour. And, of course, I was the only Inuk to ever make it there.

They divided the players into two teams, one of which was coached by Don Cherry, and the other coached by Bobby Orr. There were some great guys in the game that year—Jason Spezza, Jason Pominville, Colby Armstrong, Cory Stillman, Lukas Krajicek—all of the best draft-eligible players in Canadian junior hockey. They had a skills competition the night before the game, and I won for the hardest shot; I think my best shot was 96.1 miles per hour.

Bobby Orr was my coach. Imagine that. The greatest hockey player in the world is coaching you. He's a legend. As a small-town boy growing up watching hockey, I only knew the big names: Mario Lemieux, Wayne Gretzky, Bobby Orr. To have Orr coach me was awesome. He knew my style. I remember him telling me, "Hey, kid, play the game hard and let's get Cherry all fired up, because you're the type of player that can rattle him." I was all for that. I only knew one style of play and that was rock 'em, sock 'em hockey. Other people told me I ought to tone it down a little bit and play less physical hockey with all of the scouts around. I thought, *Fuck that—I want to rattle Grapes's team a bit. Give him a taste of his own medicine. If he likes rock 'em, sock 'em, I'll give him rock 'em, sock 'em.*

I don't know if I ever did rattle Cherry, but we beat his team 5–3 and I did get to talk to him. Hockey has taken me to a lot of places I never expected to go and let me meet people I'll never forget.

I didn't really think too much about the significance of the game. I just went out and played. I didn't hear anything about how I was ranked afterwards, which was fine. To me, less is more. But I guess I did make a bit of an impression by playing the way I play. The media asked Bobby Orr about me after the game. He said, "Is he a hard rock, or what? He's a tough kid. Everyone's always talking about size in our game, and here's one player that's not real tall, but he's just as strong as a horse. He's looked at as small because he's not 6'4". But he's one that could play in the National Hockey League. He's got a heart as big as this rink, and he plays very, very well. I was really impressed with Jordin."

Don Cherry talked about me, too. I guess it shouldn't really be a surprise that I was his kind of hockey player. "Tootoo, I wish I'd have had him in the Boston Bruins," he said. "He looks like he should have played for the old Bruins. I just think he's great, and I don't know if a lot of people know of Stan Jonathan, but he reminds me of Stan Jonathan. He's a great hockey player, and he will be in the National Hockey League, there's no doubt in my mind."

That was good to hear.

I ALREADY HAD an agent by then: Don Meehan at Newport Sports Management, who was probably the most powerful agent in the sport. Kelly McCrimmon introduced me to Don when I was fifteen, and I was with him until the summer of 2010. At the time, I didn't really understand how that part of the hockey business worked—or even who Don Meehan was. He was put in front of me and Kelly said, "This is a guy who could help you in your career." *Frick, why not? Where do I sign?* Obviously, Meehan thought I had NHL potential way back then. As for me, I knew I was a good enough player to get drafted but, other than that, I wasn't a guy who really followed that part of the game. I let my play determine my outcome and that's what happened. Scouts had come to watch me play in Brandon, but most of the communication with them was through Kelly. He'd tell me the nights when they were in the stands and even though I might have been slightly hung over, I blocked that out and turned it up a notch, knowing I was being watched.

It wasn't until a couple of weeks before the draft that I knew where I was ranked. Most of the experts were saying that I'd be picked in the third or fourth round. I didn't really care where I was picked or which team picked me. The important part for me was just having that chance.

The draft happens in June, at the end of the NHL season. That year they held it in Sunrise, Florida, where the Panthers play. Ilya Kovalchuk was the first overall pick, followed by Jason Spezza. I had stayed in Brandon after the Wheat Kings' season finished. On draft day, my parents flew down from Rankin Inlet, and Terence was there. The whole family got together at a hotel in Brandon. We had a little gathering in the lounge and then sat there for what seemed like hours, waiting for the phone to ring. After the first couple of rounds they stop showing the draft on television, so we had no idea what was going on.

Finally, my cellphone rang. It was David Poile, general manager of the Nashville Predators, telling me that they had taken me with the first pick in the fourth round, ninety-eighth overall. They actually had traded up to take me in that spot. It was only then that it hit me: *Fuck, this is really happening. I've been drafted. I'm going to play in the NHL.* My brother was there. My whole family was there. It was a special moment.

When we got back to Rankin Inlet, it was one big, big party. The first Inuk player to ever get drafted by the NHL . . . that's a pretty good excuse to light 'er up.

THAT SUMMER, I went down to Nashville for a rookie camp. I had been in the States a few times on road trips, since there are some American teams in the WHL. But it was my first experience being in the real South. When I got there, the temperature was about 90 degrees and the humidity was unbearable, at least for a northern guy like me. I'd thought the weather was going to be like it is in Winnipeg. At first I just stayed in my hotel with the AC blasting. The only time I left was for the one-minute walk to the rink.

The idea was to introduce the drafted players to the coaches, the team, and the city. That's when I first met Barry Trotz, who was the head coach of the Predators. He was a Manitoba boy, from Dauphin, who knew Kelly McCrimmon, and he welcomed me with open arms. But we actually spent most of our time with guys from their minor league system, including Claude Noël, who went on to coach the Winnipeg Jets.

Despite the heat, Nashville made an immediate impression on me. A lot of people talked about how great it was to live there and how friendly the people were. But the team was still new, and hockey wasn't all that big there. We were able to see some sights during that week. The city started growing on me right then and there. I thought about coming back and living there and experiencing the country music scene and all of that stuff.

On the hockey side, the trip was a real eye-opener. Three days before the trip, I was all pissed up, still partying after the draft. I hadn't set foot in the gym. I'd thought it was going to be fucking easy. Instead, it was a whole other level of being in shape. At that age, when you're done with hockey at the end of the season, you don't think about being in the gym. And then there was the mental part of the game. When you're playing with junior kids, the game is a lot slower. I didn't quite understand all of the systems they were talking about in Nashville. They were giving us all these booklets on things like faceoff plays. *Holy shit.* We didn't really have those in Brandon. It was more like: this is how we're going to forecheck, and this is how we're going to break out, and other than that just go out and play hockey. Rookie camp was more like going to school again for me. But I embraced the experience of being around NHL guys—guys who had been around in the league. Some of them were working out at that camp because they had kids in school in Nashville. Brent Gilchrist was there, Cliff Ronning, Tom Fitzgerald. It was pretty intimidating at first, but when you're in that environment for long enough it just becomes normal. And it was a pretty neat experience for a kid, and the first Inuk—going all the way down south and seeing the life of a pro hockey player for the first time. What I saw there told me that it was time to start changing my focus, because there was work to be done to make it to the next level.

In September, I returned to Nashville for the Predators' rookie camp. I got to play in an exhibition game, and stuck around camp longer than any of the players drafted higher than me. So I started thinking, *Fuck, I'm the man around here.* It wasn't really a surprise when they sent me back to junior. But the experience of being in an NHL camp and hanging in there for that long gave me a real boost of confidence. It set me up for a great year in Brandon.

MEANWHILE, Terence had finished up his final season with OCN and was looking for a way to continue in hockey. He had been the captain there for three years, and I think that's what really kept him in The Pas. He had an opportunity to play in The Dub but he knew that the money wasn't as good. He was good enough to play major junior, but in the back of his mind he was thinking, *I've got to get paid.* That was his mindset all through junior hockey. At the end of the day, he was playing to support our family, sending money home to shut them up.

I don't know if it was because he left home at an older age or because he didn't get the practice needed, but for whatever reason he was a step behind me in hockey, and he knew that. He told me, "You're a better player than I am. I've got to find a way to stick it out. You're younger, you know the systems and stuff, and how it works. For me, it took a little longer but I'm going to make it work."

Terence's coaches had a contact at the Roanoke Express, a team in the East Coast Hockey League that played out of Roanoke, Virginia. The ECHL is a second-tier minor league one level below the American Hockey League, so two levels below the NHL. The teams all play in the States, and most of them are affiliated with NHL teams.

The guys in Roanoke got a call about Terence and looked at his stats and decided to offer him a tryout. Terence went down there and he made the team. It's funny: just recently, I ran into a guy named Mark Bernard. He's a scout now, but in those days he was the general manager in Roanoke, the guy who gave Terence a chance there. He told me how much they loved him, how the fans there embraced his style of play. Mark told me that when he sees me play now, it's just like watching Terence. That kind of tickled me.

Terence definitely enjoyed his time in Roanoke. He wanted to be a pro and he was going to do whatever it took to move up to the next level—the American Hockey League—and then after that, who knows. Maybe a shot at the NHL. He always told me, "You may have gotten a little bit better than me, so I'm going to have to work my way up and catch you."

I don't think Terence was ever jealous of the success I enjoyed. He always encouraged me. He'd say, "I'm proud of you, keep going. You do your thing. For me, it might take a little extra time, but I'm ready for that challenge." I never saw jealousy in his eyes and he never asked why everything was happening for me and not for him.

When he got to Roanoke, he became the city's favourite hockey player right off the bat. And he enjoyed living down there. He talked about it all the time. "I'm kind of on my own here. Nothing to worry about. I'm far enough away from everyone." For him, it wasn't tough at all being away. He was doing what he loved and he was three thousand miles away from the shit at home whereas, when he was in The Pas, he was still close enough to have to deal with it.

The only problem with the ECHL was that Terence had to take a big pay cut. With OCN, Terence was making good money under the table, but in Roanoke he was making fucking peanuts. Still, he always found a way to send money home. As soon as I signed my first contract with Nashville and got my bonus money, I got a call from him. "Now it's your turn to look after the family. I'm fucking struggling here. You make sure you look after Mom and Dad."

I tried sending money to Terence, but he wouldn't take it. I told him that he had looked after me and it was time for me to pay him back, but he wouldn't accept it. He said, "I don't want any of your money." The only help he would accept was for sticks and gear. Beyond that, he didn't want to deal with money anymore. He just wanted to enjoy his life.

I HAD A GREAT SEASON in 2001–2002. By the end of the year, it was pretty obvious that I was more than just a tough guy. I finished as the Wheat Kings' leading scorer, with 32 goals and 39 assists. We finished first in our division and then beat Saskatoon and Swift Current in the playoffs before losing a tough seven-game series to Red Deer in the semifinals. Not that my game had completely changed. I had 272 penalty minutes that year, also tops on the team, and fought sixteen times. In every one of those sixteen fights, the guy I had faced was taller than me, heavier than me, or both. And that's not just my memory. There are statistics. There are actually people who keep track of stuff like that.

My confidence was pretty high. I knew that I couldn't be satisfied with just being a junior player and I had to start learning how to be a pro. I was setting goals, reaching them, and then setting new goals. It was tough for me, because I was now looked at as the go-to guy on the team. But it wasn't my teammates or coaches putting pressure on me. It was more me putting pressure on myself, and trying to prove to others that I could be a pro hockey player.

That summer, I was looking forward to going to the Predators' training camp again. I knew that it would be tough to crack an NHL roster as a nineteen-year-old, and that I'd probably return to Brandon for my final year of junior. But coming off a season like that one, I thought I had an outside chance to stick around.

And Terence was coming off a great season, too. They loved him in Roanoke, loved the way he played, and they wanted him back. But he also had an offer to try out with the Norfolk Admirals in the American Hockey League. If he made it, that would mean better money, and it would be one step closer to the NHL.

Terence was all jacked up about that. Things were really going well.

SEVEN

*I*n the summer of 2002, Terence arrived in Brandon following his first season with the Roanoke Express. On the ice, it couldn't have been a more successful debut. He had made history, becoming the first Inuk to play professional hockey, and while the first two lines of his rookie statistical record—9 goals and 16 assists—didn't suggest much, the third one did—218 penalty minutes. Though undersized, Terence was fearless, tormenting the opposition, getting under their skin, and scrapping when necessary; in other words, he played hockey the Tootoo way. In a nontraditional southern U.S. hockey market, he immediately became a fan favourite, and almost from the start number 22 Tootoo jerseys started popping up in the crowd. Though some had picked Roanoke to win a championship that season, the Express were knocked out in the first round of the ECHL playoffs. Before leaving for home, Terence ordered his sticks for the 2002–2003 season, but he was hoping to take another step forward and make the jump to the Norfolk Admirals of the American

Hockey League, then the number-one farm team of the Chicago Blackhawks. Terence had understood from the start that it would be a difficult road from hockey's low minors to the National Hockey League. But if long odds fazed the Tootoo brothers, they never would have left Rankin Inlet. And the truth was, they were closer to their dream of suiting up together in the NHL than they had ever been. Upon arriving in Brandon, Terence moved in with Jordin, sharing a basement bedroom in the home of his billets, Neil and Janene, on the outskirts of town. It was a great summer. Jordin was a junior hockey celebrity—a star in a one-sport, one-team town—the Tootoo brothers were together once again, and though the family burdens remained, they seemed far, far away. During the day, Jordin and Terence trained hard for the upcoming season and, at night, they tore up the town. On August 27, with summer quickly drawing to a close, Jordin, his girlfriend Meghan, and Terence went out to sample the Brandon nightlife as they had so many times before.

I need to tell you about my brother, Terence.

Growing up, he was always a caring guy who looked after other people before he looked after himself. I remember that as a kid, as hard as he was on me, he was always there to protect me. In the community, everybody admired him for being the way he was. He carried himself with laughter and he always had a positive vibe wherever he went. He was always so caring, and very charismatic. He wasn't a guy who said a lot. He wasn't the life of the party. He sat back quietly. But when he spoke, you listened. He never showed any negativity. Maybe that hurt him, because he couldn't express those darker feelings. Just because you always seem happy doesn't mean you're a happy person.

I was more of a daredevil. I didn't care about the consequences in the moment. Terence was a guy who thought twice and considered the worst-case scenario. He was the one who friends relied on for the right answers on anything that lay ahead. And he always had those answers. He always came through. He wasn't the biggest guy, but a lot of friends and family members looked to Terence when they had to get things done. Even if it was a two-man job, a three-man job, Terence found a way to do it by himself.

When people were around him, they would watch what he did. They followed his lead. He carried himself with a lot of confidence. Growing up, his buddies looked up to him. He was kind of the leader of the pack. He was always willing to try something new to test it out before anyone else did, just to make sure it was okay.

He was quiet, except in the dressing room. It was like he turned into a different man when he put on his hockey equipment. Growing up, he wasn't much of a talker in public, but in the dressing room he was a very vocal guy. He wasn't afraid to make speeches there, because he was in his comfort zone.

On the ice, he had the same style as I do. He was a great skater. He played hard. He wasn't afraid to drop his gloves. He caught a lot of players off guard, because he was a southpaw who shot the puck right-handed but punched left-handed.

Terence was really close to my dad—a lot closer than I was. He was his right-hand man, because he was older. He was always by Dad's side, looking after him—really, sometimes babysitting him. Out on the land, Terence was Dad's guy. He was always around to do whatever he was told to do. When my dad needed help, Terence was there. As much as he loved to stay in town on weekends, Terence sacrificed that to go out on the land with my dad. And when Dad went on a bender in town, it was Terence who went to find him.

My mother and Terence had a great relationship, too. I think my mom thought of him as her saviour. When times were tough, she leaned on his shoulders. If it wasn't for Terence, I don't think our family would be together today. When things got rough between my parents, he was the mediator. That was a lot to put on a kid. The solution was always: "Call Terence. Terence will calm things down." That's the way it was.

When Terence moved down south to play hockey, that's when things started to get really tough at home. And then when he left us, that's when all hell broke loose.

THE LAST TIME I saw Terence was that night out in Brandon. In a couple of days, he was going to be heading to Norfolk, Virginia, for his tryout with the Admirals, and so we were partying hard because I wasn't going to see him until the next summer. At the end of the night we all jumped in his vehicle, all pissed up with not a worry in the world. We'd done it a hundred times. No big deal.

We lived out in the country, fifteen minutes outside of Brandon, with our billets, Neil and Jeanine. But my girlfriend, Meghan, lived five blocks from the bar where we were.

I said, "Let's just stay at Meghan's house—spend the night here and go train in the morning."

Terence said, "No, I'm going to go home."

Being the younger brother, I wasn't going to force Terence to do anything he didn't want to do. He was always set in his ways. If he had something in mind, he was going to fucking do it. That's just the way he was. So, the plan was to meet the next morning at the Keystone Centre, the Wheat Kings' rink, to work out.

I said, "Are you sure you want to drive home? Just fucking stay here." But he left. And I guess as soon as he pulled onto the main drag, the police lights went on. I didn't see that. He had no cellphone, nothing. He got pulled over and the cops recognized who he was, because we're both well known in Brandon. They tested him and he was over the limit. They told him, "We're going to drive you home to where you're staying and we'll just leave it at that, but we're going to impound your car." Instead of taking him down to the station, they dropped him off at my billets' place at three o'clock in the morning. Neil and Jeanine were light sleepers. They always seemed to know when I came home. But I guess they didn't wake up.

The protocol is that when you drop off someone who is intoxicated, someone sober has to be there to take responsibility for the person. But it was all hush-hush that night. Because Terence was one of the Tootoos and that was a pretty recognizable name in Brandon, the cops decided to keep it quiet. Because of my popularity in Brandon and Terence's in northern Manitoba, the police tried to keep everything on the down low. All of the cops knew who we were. Heck, I was dating the police chief's daughter. They knew where I lived and decided to bring Terence to my billets' house and keep everything under wraps.

They just said, "Okay, here's your place, go ahead and we won't say anything." He went into the house and things must have been going a million miles an hour in his head. I've wondered about how I would have been thinking if I'd been pulled over—*Holy fuck, I'm supposed to go to the States in a couple of days and now I've got a DUI. They might not let me back across the border. What if I can't play hockey anymore?*

My brother must have thought his life was over. He must have been thinking, *So, fuck, this is it. All the work I've done has just gone down the drain.* And everyone would know. It would be humiliating. I think he just couldn't deal with that being in the public eye. Everyone thought that Terence was this great guy, and that's how he wanted to be perceived. Everyone makes mistakes, but for him, with all that pressure coming at him from different angles, I just don't think he had the will inside him to fight it anymore. Instead, it was like, *Fuck, this is it. I'm done. I don't want to deal with all of these people thinking I'm not this perfect, perfect guy.*

THE PLACE WE STAYED at out in the country had a gun in the garage, a 12-gauge shotgun, because we'd go out hunting in the fields behind the house all the time. As best we know, Terence went downstairs to the basement where our room was and took off all of his clothes except his underwear. He set his clothes by the bed and then wrote me a note: *Jor, go all the way. Take care of the family. You are the man. Terence.* He set the note beside the bed and walked out.

I have analyzed that letter over and over ever since. He knew I had the skill to go all the way and take care of the family. And in Brandon, any time we were out in public, everyone was all over me—so his last line was "You are the man." I felt bad, but I didn't mean to be the man—it just kind of happened. He had to have been incoherent. Fricking blacked out. He couldn't have known what the hell was going on. It was kind of chilly that night, but he went out in just his underwear—no shoes or nothing.

He went to the garage and grabbed three shells and the 12-gauge. Then he walked down to where there was a little trail. There was a fence there. He jumped the fence and fired off one shot there, into the air. I don't know how Neil and Jeanine didn't wake up. Then he put the second shell in, pulled the trigger, and it only clicked. It misfired. But he was so determined. Then he put the third shell in. That was it.

WHY DID HE DO IT? I've gone back over all the details a million times, what happened with the police and all the other stuff. We'll never know the whole answer. My parents talked about suing the police, but I wasn't involved in a lot of that. I do know that the officers involved were questioned and then formally admonished, but as far as I know that was it. I can't speak on behalf of my parents about what exactly they were fighting for. I understand that you feel you need someone to blame, but from my perspective, when it's suicide, you can't blame anyone because you're being selfish, you're thinking of only you, and it only creates more problems.

There's a lot of suicide in Rankin Inlet, and in other northern and First Nations communities. I understand the part about the lifestyle up there, and being isolated, and feeling that there's nothing out there, so fuck it. It happens all the time. Part of Terence taking his own life had to do with feeling like he didn't matter, like he was no big deal. And then there are all of the extracurricular activities: booze and drugs. There's nothing else there. People think they've got nothing else to give, so *Fuck it, I'm done.* A lot of young kids, a lot of these ten-, twelve-, and thirteen-year-old kids grew up the same way we grew up. Their families are very dysfunctional and booze is the biggest reason for that. It's like a fucking switch is flipped. I've seen it first-hand. And those kids want a way out.

But with Terence, it was also about all of those years spent putting up with shit and being a role model, and then letting people down. He must have said, *I'm spent. My hockey career's done and what else have I got?* And my brother was fed up with all of the bullshit he had to deal with at home—picking Dad up when he was drunk, breaking up fights, seeing shit being thrown around the house. He was the middleman and I was the kid sitting in the corner watching all of this shit going on.

We'd wake up the next day and, for my parents, it was like it had never happened. You absorb all that. In the end, I think part of Terence's reasoning for taking his own life is that he didn't want to deal with that shit anymore. Having Mom calling or Dad doing something terrible, having to be the mediator. He was a young kid himself, but at the same time he was like a fucking counsellor, a person stuck in the middle who can't be a kid when he wants to be. And now here he was an adult, still sending his hockey paycheques home to Mom.

Terence wasn't an outspoken person. He was a guy who held in a lot. He's the same way my father is—he holds in a lot of his anger and his frustration until he has a few cocktails and then it just starts coming out. Terence was the spitting image of my father in that way. He loved to party, and he was a fucking great guy, but he partied for all the wrong reasons. He partied to get drunk. That day, he was drunk and he got pulled over by the cops and it was like, *Fuck this—I've let everyone down. My parents. The people of Nunavut. This is my only way out.* He was depressed and fed up, but he didn't want to show that weakness because he was the older brother. He was the first pro Inuk player, a big role model for everyone, and he didn't want to show any weakness. And you know, that's how my dad is— you're never going to see him show any weakness. If he's sad, he's never going to cry. They always say a true man cries, but no one has ever seen my dad do that. His job is to make sure that everyone else is looked after and that everything is going to be okay. And that was Terence.

At the end of the day, suicide is selfish. You will never know what really leads to a suicide. You can speculate all you want. But I was with him until the bitter last hours before he took his life, and I never knew he was hurting inside because he never showed it.

THE NEXT DAY I woke up at my girlfriend's place around ten o'clock and called the house. There was no answer. No one was around. Neil and Jeanine had gone to work. I figured that Terence must have fricking passed out because he was so blitzed. I went to the rink at eleven and he wasn't there. Again, I figured he was pretty tanked the night before, so he was probably still sleeping.

So I went to work out and got home around 12:30. I saw his shoes there. I went downstairs and his clothes were there. And the note was there. I read it real quick and thought, *What the hell is this?* But I didn't think anything more of it than that. I crumpled it up and threw it in the garbage. (After all was said and done, the Brandon Police picked up the note. I don't know what happened to it after that.) The only thing I was thinking was, *Where the fuck is he? Where's his truck?*

It was mid-afternoon when Neil called me and told me that the Brandon Police had called to tell him that Terence had got a DUI the night before, and that his car had been impounded. What the fuck? But there were no text messages from him. No phone calls.

That's when I began looking for him. I thought that maybe he took off to the States on a bus or something, or just got out of

Dodge to get away from everyone. Get across the border before all the shenanigans went down. So I called all of the bus stations, but there was no record of him. By then it was six o'clock at night. I was wondering, *Where the fuck did he go? He must have bolted town.* That's what I was thinking. Then Neil came to me and said, "I hate to ask, but you know the gun you always use when you go out hunting? Have you seen it?" I checked the garage. No gun. Fuck. But we used to hunt geese out back all the time, or just go out there to shoot the gun. So he could have been doing that.

By then, it was getting dark out. Neil and I hopped the fence. We walked around calling his name: "Ter, are you here?" Nothing. We did that for at least half an hour. Nothing. That's when we called the Brandon Police and told them we had a missing person. I told them exactly what I thought: that he was probably out in the bush somewhere. The gun was gone. They said they'd bring the search dogs.

We had been out there just an hour before, so the dogs picked up our scent first and followed it for fifteen or twenty minutes and didn't find anything. We had a meeting with the cops and they said they'd come back the next day after our scent was gone because Terence was definitely out there somewhere, and he had the gun.

They came back at seven the next morning. They hopped the fence and the dogs started going apeshit. It was still kind of dark. I was standing by the garage with Kelly McCrimmon. Neil went over the fence to take a look. Then all I could hear was his screaming. I just fainted into Kelly's arms.

The night before, if I had looked to my right, five feet into the bush, it would have been me who found him. Thank God, I didn't.

All that time, right up until we found Terence, I never thought that he would have killed himself. It didn't even cross my mind. Never. That was the last thing I would have thought. He loved hunting and, you know, Terence was a survivor. He was a guy who could fucking rough it. In my mind, I was thinking, *Well, he's probably built a little hut back there, he's trying to hide, to hide from everyone.* That's what I was thinking.

By that time my parents were in the air flying to Winnipeg, because I'd called them and said, "Hey, look, I don't know where Terence is." They'd jumped on a plane that got in at ten o'clock in the morning and we found him at seven. It's a two and a half-hour drive from Brandon to Winnipeg. Kelly, Neil, and I made the trip.

At the airport, they have a quiet room where they bring people when there's trouble. When my parents arrived, all hell just broke loose in there.

The drive back to Brandon was a bit of a blur. My mom was so out of it, we thought she might have to be hospitalized. When we got there, she wanted to identify the body to make sure it was Terence. I eventually convinced her not to see him. Neil went in to identify him. I wanted our last memories of Terence to be of when he was happy—not of what he did to himself, not of the way he was then.

Eventually, we cremated him. They ask you what kind of clothes you want him to wear for the last time. I picked out his clothes. Terence was a casual guy, a T-shirt and jeans guy. I picked out a nice plaid shirt that I remembered him wearing.

SINCE THAT DAY, it's been hell for my parents. You can see in their eyes that they're still hurting. Every day, I think of Terence, but for me it's joyful now. It's not that I'm over his death, but I understand that I have to move on. But for them—they're still in pain. I can't imagine being a parent and losing a kid.

My dad's never, ever going to show emotion about it, though. That's just how he is. And my mom is my mom. She's going to be that way forever. I've tried to help them get professional help and stuff, but they're not interested. They don't want to talk about it. That's how they grew up. It's frowned upon. Any unpleasant issues, any issues at all, nothing was talked about. Communication was very minimal. And even to this day, when I try to ask questions about certain situations, it's as if they're on the defensive. It's as if I'm always walking a fine line with both of my parents.

At some point you have to get over losing someone, but my parents haven't. They talk like they have, but once they start drinking, that's when everything comes out. I understand that. I understand that perspective. I've told my mom that I can't imagine what it must be like for her. But it's been over ten years now. You have to embrace Terence's life and let his memory live on. But to them, it's an issue. They say I don't understand, and that's an easy way out, an excuse.

I had to ask my parents some questions about Terence and how he was brought up. They got their backs up. *Why the fuck are you asking us? Why do you need to know?* I ask my mom questions and she says, "Don't ever fucking ask me questions like that again. Don't you ever fucking bring up shit like that again." They weren't even direct questions. You've got to kind of work around things with my parents. You're walking a fine line. You don't want my mom to snap because you don't know what's going to happen. And you know, as a child, that you don't ever want to see your parents hurt themselves or your siblings. That's the fine line I'm walking every day. My dad pushes my mom to the brink of taking her own life some days, and she talks about suicide and it's like, *Holy fuck, what the fuck is going on?*

So, for our family, the truth is that it's been hell. It's tough sometimes for my parents when they're lonely. I think Terence's death is something they're never, ever going to let go of. Terence was their pride and joy.

Back home, they still keep his room just like it was when he was alive. Obviously, we have a lot of great memories and that's what we've got to embrace. I walk into his room all the time when I'm alone, and I look at all the old pictures and hold his trophies and all his medals and stuff like that. It brings me joy, because it's something that will never be taken away from me.

ONE OF THE QUESTIONS I had to ask my parents was about Terence's ashes. My understanding was that, after we cremated him, the ashes were going to be spread on the land near our cabin. But nothing was ever said as to when this was going to be done. I thought there would be a little ceremony, but I never heard anything more about it, and just assumed that whatever was said had been done. But nothing ever came up about it. So I had to get that straight. I finally asked them directly: "What did you do with Terence's ashes?"

My mom said, "We still have them."

"What? I thought you guys were going to spread his ashes out by our cabin."

"No, I still have them up in our room."

I went to their room with my sister and saw the box, and we had a little conversation about the whole situation. Corinne said we couldn't tell them what to do. But, as a family, we should be able to have a ceremony about letting him go and having his spirit in our hearts. The whole thing kind of rattled me.

I understand from a parent's perspective that it's hard to let go. But my parents go to bed and his ashes are still right there in their bedroom. It's something you've got to be able to let go of. For my parents—for my mom, especially—it's hard. And that's holding her back and causing a lot more stress in her life. It's kind of sad to see. She uses anger as a coping mechanism. And that's not how it should be. You can't keep going back to something that's in the past.

I've talked to her a bit about it. She tells me I don't understand the pain it causes her. It's just the same story over and over again. It's not that I'm completely over the whole situation. But I'm not a parent.

TWO WEEKS AFTER Terence died, I was back with the Wheat Kings. Terence always told me that he wanted me to do what I loved, and so I felt like that was the right place for me to be. I wanted to stick to our goal. We loved playing hockey. When I decided to keep playing, I think I really got a lot of respect from my parents. I was at a point in my career when I could have just fucking said I'm done, called it quits, and that's it—and have had something to blame it on. But that's not what Terence would have wanted. He would want me to be doing what I love, so that's what I did.

I was angry early on, for sure. But you can't dwell on it. You can't keep asking yourself those questions because, fuck, you just get so wrapped up in it. It consumes you. It's not that it's wasted energy, but it's energy you know at some point you have to put somewhere else. For me, it's not so much a daily battle as a daily, constant reminder of how important life is.

I went back over the night that Terence died all the time—for five years. But I would do it only when I was partying, when I was alone at night all pissed up. That's when I would start thinking. And then I'd have another shot to try to put me out of my misery, to pass out. Or I would use women to keep my mind off of it. I needed that to help release the weight off my shoulders. For many years I blamed myself for Terence's death. What could I have done? Why didn't I do this or that? Why was I partying so much with him? When my mind started getting clearer I realized that if you grow up with physical and mental abuse, you have to deal with it.

EIGHT

Despondent after Terence's suicide, Jordin had little time to grieve. He was a draft pick of the Nashville Predators, and they expected him at their pre-season training camp within days. If he didn't stick with the National Hockey League team, he'd be back playing junior hockey in Brandon, and living in the same place where his brother had spent his final hours. For a brief moment, Jordin considered giving up the game altogether, giving up his dream, and heading back to Rankin Inlet. But then he thought of the words in Terence's note, and understood that he had to go on.

Hockey became an outlet for me, something I could use to numb all of my pain and help me forget about it. When Terence passed away at the end of August, training camp was just starting in Nashville. A few days went by, and I remember telling my dad, "I need to be on the ice. I need to go." There were optional skates for the Wheat Kings players in Brandon and I started there, and then I took off for Nashville.

Terence's death had been publicized, so everybody knew about it. Obviously, suicide is a touchy subject. But the Predators organization was great to me. They gave me all kinds of extra support. If I needed to talk to anyone, at any time, they were available. Barry Trotz was a big part of that. He was probably the first guy to sit me down and sincerely ask me if there was anything he could do; he was almost in tears. He didn't want anything bad to happen to me. He and David Poile, they really cared about me as a person. That's very hard to come by. You don't find people like that in the hockey business these days. It really made me feel comfortable seeing that these people who didn't even know me—and who I didn't know—cared about me so much. Everyone came up to me and said, "Here's my number; call if you need anything." It was like that, and it's still like that to this day with the friends I made on that team.

I played in a few exhibition games during camp, and then they sent me back to Brandon, which is what I expected would happen. It was all kind of a blur to me. Returning to Brandon was just unbelievable. The city really embraced me. I don't think I've ever heard anyone cheer louder than the city of Brandon when I came back to play my first game after Terence's death.

That could have been the point when I called it quits and said, *Fuck it, I don't want to play hockey anymore.* It would have been an easy out: I don't want to play hockey because I lost my brother. But I knew that Terence would have wanted me to keep going. He said so in the note he left for me. Every time I stepped onto the ice, I just felt the presence of my brother, his spirit.

FROM THE FIRST GAME of the season in Brandon, when the crowd gave me that great welcome, until the beginning of December, I was fucking on fire. I scored 5 points in my first game back, and in the first 35 games of the season I had 25 goals and 57 points. I was the leading goal scorer in the whole league. The WHL is a tough place, and there I was, a guy who was only supposed to be a fighter, ahead of everyone in points. I was playing unreal hockey, and that gave me a legitimate shot at playing for Team Canada in the World Junior Championship, which was being held in Halifax at the end of that year.

The season before, I'd been invited to the evaluation camp for the World Juniors but hadn't made the team. This time it was a no-brainer. I was the best player in the league, playing on the first line for the Wheat Kings. I went to the World Juniors camp and played a few exhibition games, and I was crushing guys while staying out of the penalty box. I started out in the fourth or fifth line in the camp rotation, but as I started to light it up—and the fans loved it—I moved up the ladder. By the last couple of days of training camp, when they'd make the final cuts, I knew I had a pretty good chance of making the team.

My roommate at that camp was Derek Roy, who played junior hockey with the Kitchener Rangers and who had been drafted by the Buffalo Sabres. We both watched as players got cut and went home. Finally, it was the last day, when the final cuts would be made and the team would be named, and we were still there. They told us we'd get a phone call.

I'll never forget that day. We woke up at six o'clock in the morning, because we knew that they always deliver the news, good or bad, really early. The phone in the hotel room rang at about 6:45. I look at Roysy and said, "Do you want to pick it up?"

He said, "No, you pick it up."

That's how nervous we were. So I picked up the phone and it was the coach, Marc Habscheid. "Is this Toots or Roysy?" he asked.

"It's Toots," I told him.

"Congratulations. You've made the team."

I was all smiles. And then he asked to talk to Roysy. It was a little tense there for a second, until he found out that he'd made the team, too. We started fist-pumping at each other and hooting and hollering. What a great feeling.

That tournament changed everything for me. I played at a level I had never played at before, and the hockey world noticed. I think that without that tournament, people across Canada would never have gotten to know me the way they did. I was a great story—an Inuk kid from the Far North, playing for Canada—and it became national news. And, of course, for the territory of Nunavut it was a big fucking deal, having one of its own guys playing for Team Canada. As a tribute, I wrote the word "Nunavut" on the sticks I used in the tournament games. And I could feel Terence looking down at me the whole time.

I remember thinking that he would have been there. He would have left his junior team to come and watch the games because that's how proud he would have been of me.

Our team had a great lineup. Out of that whole group, I think there are only seven guys now who haven't played in the NHL. Marc-André Fleury was the number-one goalie and he had a fantastic tournament. And then there were Joffrey Lupul, Kyle Wellwood, Carlo Colaiacovo, and a bunch of others. A lot of them were guys I had played against already—or would play against later in my career—and we still run into each other and share that bond. That's one of the things that's great about the hockey world. Those relationships last. You can be friends with a guy you played with in juniors and see him ten years later and you don't miss a beat. It's a pretty special feeling.

The other teams had some future stars, too—including a seventeen-year-old playing for Russia who no one had ever heard of before named Alexander Ovechkin.

But frick, we were just kids back then. The shit that we did. . . . We were horny young men. We were in Halifax and we had every goddamned girl hitting on us. What are you going to do? *Let's start slaying these broads.* And it wasn't just one-on-one action. A few of the guys would get a couple of girls after practice and head into one of the rooms. Enough said.

At the beginning of the tournament I don't think any of us really realized what was at stake, and how much pressure there was on us to win. I didn't really understand that until after the gold-medal game. We went undefeated through the preliminary round and then beat the Americans 3–2 in the semifinals.

The Russians were undefeated as well when we met them in the finals. Of course, Canada versus Russia has been the big hockey rivalry going all the way back to 1972. It felt like the whole country was watching us.

It was nuts in the arena. When we scored a goal, I thought my eardrums were going to explode. We were up 2–1 going into the third period. The boys were pretty relaxed. But then— *boom, boom*—the Russians scored two goals and it was all over. We lost 3–2.

I was on the ice for the last shift of the game. I'll never forget looking over at my best friend, Scottie Upshall, right after the game ended. He was the captain of that team. He'd scored the second goal of the game. I'd known him since Spruce Grove, when we'd played on a select team together. We have been buddies ever since. The game was over, we'd lost, and Scottie was bawling his eyes out. *Holy fuck.* That's when I realized that we'd let this game slip away in our home country. I had never seen Scottie like that, before or since. It's heartbreaking, as a teenage kid, to let your country down. You're playing in the biggest tournament of your life. All of that raw emotion from the fans is just pouring down on you and then that buzzer goes off and you realize that you've failed—not only failed your teammates, but failed your country.

Everyone remembers how the Russians celebrated—on *our* turf. I was standing on the ice, watching them, and then looking at the other guys on our team. No one had to say it. We were thinking, *Fuck these guys. Let's fucking beat them up right now.* I

I may be the first Inuk to make it to the NHL, but my people have been making a living on the ice for a long time. Above is my father beside a muskox he brought down. Below is my first regular-season fight in the NHL, against Mike Danton. Life on the ice can be dangerous and you have to respect that. But you never show fear.

My family has always meant the world to me. The people around you are the people who shape who you are. Above are my parents at their wedding. To the right are the three of us kids in the kitchen in Rankin. That's Terence on the left and Corinne on the right. I'm the little guy in the middle. And below, that's the three of us, all grown up, at Corinne's wedding.

You don't get anywhere in life without dreaming. Here I am (above) as a little kid just thrilled to be playing minor hockey on indoor ice. Below, I'm standing on the blue line in Halifax as part of Team Canada. To be identified as a guy who can help the best players in the country win gold is an unbelievable honour.

I think about my big brother every day. Growing up, he always had my back. I cherished my time playing junior hockey with him as well. Even though we were far from home, we were together almost around the clock. We always had the same dream, and that is something I still think about.

You know you have a problem when what you're doing off the ice affects your job. I took things to extremes in the bars in Nashville, and while I could still mix it up when the puck dropped, I knew I was not the hockey player I could have been back then.

When my contract was up in Nashville, I felt it was time to leave. But I always remained grateful to the Predators, both for drafting me and supporting me during a dark time. Below is coach Barry Trotz with my parents. For whatever reason, I never felt like a close-knit part of the team in Detroit. It can be tough to play an emotional game like hockey at its highest level when the bonds aren't as close.

I have been through some tough times, but I never lose sight of how lucky I am. I have some great friends and family. That's me with my old teammate Scottie Upshall, back when we were teammates in Nashville (above) and with Brian McGrattan at my wedding (right). Most important, I was lucky enough to get married in the summer of 2014. That's me with Jennifer on our wedding day, with my mother and father.

Life as a pro hockey player isn't all glamour, but it does mean eating at fancy restaurants and flying on chartered jets. None of that ever distracted me from what is important in life. For me, that means the land and the people who matter to you—and the two go together. That's me and my father fishing on the ice (above). And below, that's me and Terence. I miss him every day.

know that was my instinct. *Look at this fucking donkey riding his stick down the ice. Fuck him.* But I had to keep it together because if I did something stupid, that would be it for me ever representing Canada again.

If that had happened in a normal junior game, that guy riding his stick would have wound up in the hospital.

My popularity blew up after that tournament. I only scored one goal and one assist, but all the reporters said that I was the fans' favourite Canadian player because of the style of hockey I played, because I would hit anything that moved. Things just skyrocketed from there and carried over into the rest of the season with the Wheat Kings. Suddenly my name was all over the place. I was crushing guys left and right, playing good old Canadian hockey, and the people in the arena and watching on television loved it. It felt like it happened overnight. The nation of Canada took me under its wing and I rode that wave for the whole two weeks of the tournament. Everywhere I went, people were praising me. I said, "Okay, relax, I'm just a regular guy like anyone else."

That was by far the highlight of my career thus far: being part of Team Canada and that whole experience. No one can ever take that away from me. I can tell my kids one day that I represented this great country. We didn't win the gold medal but that didn't change the way people felt about me. That tournament really put my name on the map, and Tootoo became a household name in a lot of places.

WHEN I RETURNED to Brandon after the tournament, it felt like everything had changed. In every arena I played in after the World Juniors, every barn in The Dub, people were applauding me, even when I was on the visiting team. Fans would stand around waiting for me after games. Oh my God, it was unbelievable. I was getting gifts from other teams, congratulating me, when the Wheat Kings would go to their rink to play them. It was amazing.

But the best reaction came from other First Nations people. I remember going to play in Prince Albert, Saskatchewan, and three-quarters of their fans were Aboriginal people from the reserves around there. They gave me a gift from the reserve; it was one of their traditional blankets with some special designs on it, plus some sweetgrass. When I scored a goal the place erupted, even though I was playing for the Wheat Kings. After the game there were so many fans waiting around our bus that we needed extra security. I was fucking loving it.

I'm very thankful to have a following like that among Aboriginal people. I can't really express those feelings in words. The way I like to say thank-you to them is to actually visit them and make time to sign autographs until the last person has got his autograph or picture. I don't want people to be shy to come up to me. This profession doesn't last forever and those kinds of things don't last forever. I want to enjoy it while it's happening and thank the Aboriginal people for letting me be a role model to them. Little do they know that they're what inspires me. I want to be a better professional for them, both on and off the ice.

I'm an Inuk, but I identify strongly with all First Nations

people. I think there are a lot of similarities among us, no matter what part of the country we come from. We are very loyal to our traditions, our culture, and our people. We're small town–oriented individuals who have a simple life and enjoy it, rather than having all of these materialistic things. We draw a lot from our roots. When I go to these Aboriginal communities and reserves, those are the similarities I see to the place where I grew up.

I'm not really a political person but I do believe that First Nations people run as one, and we just want to be treated equally. It doesn't matter what colour skin you have or where you come from. We're all human beings and we want to be treated the way everyone should be treated—and that's fairly and equally, and not being judged.

IT WASN'T JUST the hockey fans in Canada who noticed me during the World Juniors tournament. I also grabbed the attention of David Poile, the general manager in Nashville, and the Predators coaching staff. They already liked me enough to have drafted me and they had liked what they saw of me in training camp. But I think that when they saw me in the tournament, it gave them an entirely different sense of my potential, of what kind of player I could be in the NHL. I won't say it was a no-brainer for the Preds to give me every opportunity to make the team the following year just because of that tournament, but they definitely saw something there and that carried over to camp the next fall.

I finished the season in Brandon with 74 points in 51 games—tied for the team lead even though I missed a bunch of time because of the World Juniors. I also had 216 penalty minutes, which was a lot, but there were guys in the league with way more than that. I was learning to control when I fought and when I didn't fight, to make better decisions, which made me a more valuable player. If you look at my statistics, I was a plus-13 that year. That tells you how much I was contributing.

I was a leader on that team. I'm not the most vocal guy, but I try to lead by example. Being a leader means that, when times are tough, your teammates need to be able to lean on you and be open to talking about issues. This applies not just in the hockey world but away from hockey as well. Not every player has the balls to go up to the coach and talk about certain situations. That's what your leaders are for. I admit I wasn't the greatest at the vocal part. Other guys like Ryan Craig and Brett Thurston played that role. But my teammates always knew where to find me when we were on the ice and things got tough.

We won our division, but were beaten by Red Deer in the third round of the playoffs. Those were great teams in Brandon, but it always seemed like we couldn't get past Red Deer. We were up 3–1 in that series. That's when I broke my first rib—right underneath my collarbone. It was just a freak accident. In game five I kind of swiped at a guy behind our net and it just popped. After the game, we were jumping on the bus to head back to Red Deer and I was in fricking pain. I could barely breathe. But I ended up fighting through it and playing through it. I wasn't 100 percent but I didn't want to let my teammates down, so I didn't say anything about it to anyone. It was a battle. But that's what makes the playoffs fun. I went to the doctors after the series and they said, "Gee, you were pretty lucky. If that bone had actually cracked, it probably would have cut one of your main arteries and you would have been done in two minutes—and you wouldn't even have known what hit you." It was a surreal moment, hearing that. Thank God that didn't happen.

NINE

*T*he Nashville Predators came into existence in 1998, part of the National Hockey League's expansion into nontraditional markets that began way back in 1967 but really gained momentum after Wayne Gretzky's trade from the Edmonton Oilers to the Los Angeles Kings in 1988. In no way was Nashville hockey country. Culturally, the city is known the world over as the capital of country music and the home of the Grand Ole Opry. As well, in the state of Tennessee, football is the sport of choice, especially the college game. Most of the fans who came out to see the Predators had never played hockey and didn't understand its finer points or its history. But they liked the speed, they liked the action, and they especially liked the rough stuff. It was a very different place than Rankin Inlet, or Brandon, but in many ways, for Jordin, Nashville was the perfect fit, both as a player and as a person.

I went to the Predators' summer prospects camp in July 2003, after my fourth season with the Wheat Kings. It's a chance for the young players to get in some extra work and get comfortable before the main training camp begins in September. You can continue playing junior hockey as an overage twenty-year-old, but I was done with it. At that point, I didn't really know whether I had a shot to make the NHL or whether I would wind up playing for the Predators' farm team in the American Hockey League, the Milwaukee Admirals.

Not long after I left Nashville at the end of prospects camp, I got a call from David Poile asking me if I would be interested in coming back down three weeks before the regular training camp began to train with their conditioning people. Of course, I said yes. I moved down on August 10 and went right into working out and pounding the weights like I never had before. By the time training camp came around, I had probably put on ten pounds of muscle.

In camp, David Poile told me just to play my game. He said, "We brought you in because of the element you bring," and I knew what that meant. So I lit 'er up, I had a couple of fights, and obviously I made an impression. Everything just kind of fell into place for me. They had a player named Scott Walker who was at the end of his career and who played the same style as I did, and he didn't really want to be that guy anymore—the energy guy, the fighter. He was done with it. And that role fit me like a glove.

I thought for sure I would have to fight Scott Walker in camp to prove a point and try to take that job for myself. Mentally, I was draining myself thinking about it. But one of the veteran players, Jim McKenzie, told me to take it easy in camp. "Don't fight your own guys in camp to make a point. You do that during exhibition games when we're playing someone else. You're not going to prove anything here by taking on veteran guys who have been around for a while." That lifted some weight off my shoulders. I didn't want to get off to a bad start with these guys by running around and being an idiot. It was nice to hear it straight up.

Jim was really important to me that year. I was a kid that came from nowhere and he was a small-town boy from Gull Lake, Saskatchewan, so we had that in common. But he had been around forever. Before he got to Nashville, he had played for eight other NHL teams—Hartford, Dallas, Pittsburgh, Winnipeg, Phoenix, Anaheim, Washington, and New Jersey— going all the way back to 1990 and he'd won a Stanley Cup the year before with the New Jersey Devils. That year in Nashville turned out to be his last season. He had been a brawler back in the day, as you can see from his numbers; in junior, he had 100 points total—and 1739 penalty minutes.

When I first moved to Nashville, Jim took me under his wing. We played a similar role, except that he was a true heavy-weight and I was a smaller guy, new to the league, and didn't know a whole lot about playing in the NHL. He really mentored me and groomed me in terms of how to be a good professional, an everyday player. He taught me that even though there are days when you're not feeling too well and you don't want to be in the gym, you have to do that extra work because that's what helps you overcome obstacles and become a champion.

I told Jim a lot about my life away from hockey. He was one of the people who really cared about me. His family was great to me, too; they had me over for dinner all the time. Jim became my roommate on the road, and I'll never forget my first trip to New York City. We went out to grab dinner and a coffee, and somehow we got separated in the crowds on the street. I was people-watching, soaking it all in, and I wasn't paying a whole lot of attention. Suddenly, I looked up and he wasn't there. Then I saw him off in the distance, obviously looking around for me and seeming distressed. When I caught up with him, I could tell he was relieved. "You scared the living daylights out of me," he said. "This is your first time here and I didn't want you to go missing. I was looking everywhere for my little Mohican." I'll never forget that that's what he called me: "my little Mohican."

Jim and I had the same mentality. Just because we were making all of this money and playing in the NHL, we didn't take it for granted. Even when you don't feel like it, when the fans are all over you, you have to embrace the opportunity. To this day, I will stay and sign autographs until the last person is happy rather than flipping the fans off the way some guys do. Jim taught me to stay until the end. Because it's not going to last forever.

On the ice, Jim taught me how to use my style and to play smart. He'd say, "On this shift, dump it in and chase it around. Let's stir it up." When he was on the ice with me, I had someone to look after me if one of our opponent's big guys came after me. He was right there. We went out and caused chaos. The guys on the bench loved it. We wouldn't take any penalties, and we were back in the game.

I learned an important lesson from veteran players like Jim. You need to be an impact player every night. But that isn't the same as needing to fight every night. The job was to go out there, cause havoc, and draw penalties. In the NHL, that became the most important part of my game.

I'm not a talker on the ice. I don't make guys mad by chirping at them. I do it physically. I give them a little jab, a tap on the back of the legs. When they are skating off the bench, I give them an extra nudge. The little fucking shit that drives them crazy. Just chipping away at them. Then instead of saying something, I just smile in silence. That drives them even more crazy.

I know what's going on. I have a game plan in my head. You play within the coach's system, but you have your own game plan, and you add to it piece by piece. I want that guy to go nuts, retaliate, and wind up in the penalty box, giving us a power play.

Some games, do I want to do that shit? Fuck, no. Let me play. But if that's what's going to keep me around, that's what I've got to do. I would take a run at somebody, wait until he knocked me down in retaliation, and then blow up to make sure the referee saw it. It doesn't make me the most popular player in the league—probably pretty close to the opposite—but it works.

I GUESS I DID enough things right during that Predators' camp, because near the end David Poile called me into his office and said, "Congratulations. You made the roster."

I had been confident. I didn't think they could send me down the way I'd played. But still, that's the kind of news you've got to hear twice before it sinks in. *What? Really? I made it? I'm in the NHL?*

Holy fuck.

BARRY TROTZ, who moved to the Capitals in 2014 and had been the longest-serving coach with one team in the NHL, really understood me from day one. We had a strong personal connection because his father was an alcoholic and he saw signs of alcoholism in my family and knew what I was dealing with. We had a lot of conversations about our families. When things started getting pretty dark with me, I was in his office quite a bit. He would tell me, "You've got to figure this out. I've seen this in my own family." He really cared about me. And maybe at that age, I didn't fully understand what he was trying to do. I was more likely to be thinking, *Fuck, why is he hounding me all the time? I'm doing everything I'm supposed to do on the ice. Why is he on me?* It never occurred to me then that he was trying to help me, that he cared about my health and was worried about what I was doing away from rink.

The truth is, he had a lot to worry about. After all of those years spent living with billet families in junior hockey, when I still found ways to do pretty much whatever I wanted to do, here I was living on my own in a condo, with no curfews, no restrictions, and a lot money in my pocket. I remember when my first NHL paycheque came in and it was like, *Holy fuck*—I think it was for $26,000. I took a picture of it and sent it to a few of my buddies. All of the years of getting paid shit money just disappeared.

The first game of the season was scheduled for October 9 against the Mighty Ducks of Anaheim (now the Anaheim Ducks). A whole crowd came down from Rankin Inlet. All of my immediate family made the trip, my sister Corinne and her husband, all of my relatives and friends that I grew up with. Even the premier of Nunavut came to the game. They had a couple of buses full of people who made the drive all the way down from Manitoba. That's not a short trip. By the time the game started, they had filled pretty much a whole section in the Nashville arena.

It was an intense week or so. The night before the game, I went out for dinner with my immediate family. My dad said, "You've been doing this all of your life. I just want you to go out there and don't think about trying to impress your family and your friends. Just go out there and do your job and have fun, make sure that you look after yourself." During the morning skate on the day of the first game, I was jumpy. The time came for my pre-game nap and I couldn't fucking sleep. This was the cream of the crop, the best league in the world. And there I was, twenty years old and getting my shot.

I got a lot of media coverage that year; really, I was the talk of the whole training camp. The press in Nashville loved my story, so by the time we got to the first game the Predators fans knew all about me, about Terence, and about where I came from. The crowd was ready for me. I jumped over the boards for my first shift and the whole arena gave me a standing ovation. It was a pretty cool moment: the first Inuk player in an NHL game— way down in the U.S. South, no less—and they were standing and cheering for me. The place kind of erupted, and it kept erupting for me as the years went on.

I was nervous. I stepped out for my first shift of the game and immediately missed a glorious chance right in the slot. The fucking puck came right to me and then it caught a rut in the ice just as I was teeing it up and bounced over my stick. I actually didn't get my first goal until about a quarter of the way through the season, at a game in Atlanta. I remember it was a one-timer, and at first I didn't even know that I'd scored the goal. I took a shot from the top of the circle and there were a bunch of guys in front of the net but somehow it went in. All of the guys were saying, "It's Tootoo's goal, we didn't touch it." They really wanted me to get that first one.

Those first few weeks in the league were amazing. But there were also times when it was pretty rough. I remember going to St. Louis for the first time. The Blues were our big rivals then, and they had Mike Danton on their roster. You probably know his story: he went to jail for trying to have his agent, David Frost, murdered, though there was a whole lot more to it than that. But at that time, he was known mostly as a fighter, kind of a crazy fighter. And I knew that going into the game. Because I was the new fighter on the Predators, I was going to be expected to take him on. For fighters, thinking about what's coming eats away at your state of mind—knowing that you're going to have to go to war, that you have to accept the challenge. That's the difference between someone a team can count on and someone they can't: being willing. As a rookie, I was trying to win the trust of my teammates. I wanted them to know I would go to war with this guy for them any day of the week. I wanted to prove myself. But I was also only twenty years old, fighting men.

I remember skating out for warm-ups that night and seeing Danton, just seeing the look in his eyes—the look that said, *I don't give a shit what happens to me; you're not going to beat me up.* I trusted my own strength but there we were looking over at each other and he had a glare in his eyes that said, *I'm going to fucking kill you.* Holy shit, that kind of intimidated me—this guy with his history and he has nothing to lose. I was nervous as hell. But that fear factor is part of what motivates me. Knowing that this was it, this was my time. I thrive in those moments. That's when you have to believe in yourself. Any time you have any doubt in your mind, you're screwed.

The warm-up seemed to take forever, and then there was the anthem. Those seconds seemed like hours. *Let's fucking get this over with.* Finally, they dropped the puck and we dropped our gloves, right off the faceoff. I fought Danton a couple of times that night, and held my ground. After that, I could feel the respect I had gained from my teammates, and from the other fighters around the league. I had showed them I wasn't afraid of anybody.

OF COURSE, I FOUGHT during that first season in Nashville, during every season before, and during every season since. Fighting was always part of my game, and it's one of the skills that got me to the NHL. The truth is, I've been fighting all of my life, one way or another. In hockey, I started fighting way back—when I was twelve or thirteen years old. Even playing street hockey, there was the odd time it boiled over. That's just how it was when I was growing up.

I know my role and it is being energetic and changing the pace of the game and dropping the gloves when that makes sense. With my style of play, I know fights are bound to happen. Someone is going to get pissed at me. If you lay a guy out, your instincts are to drop the gloves. I did that for the first seven years of my NHL career. I went out looking for it.

Nowadays, it's a little different. I pick my spots. I fight on my terms. I fight when my team needs it. I'm not going to fight on anybody else's terms. If a fight arises, it arises. I don't go looking for fights. But then, sometimes, something goes down and it becomes your job to fight. You get a tap on the shoulder from the coach and you know what you're supposed to do. I think now I have a better understanding of when it's time to change the momentum in the game with a fight. It's about communicating with the guys on your team. Sometimes the guys need a lift, and you get out there and create it. You don't have to say to the other guy, "Do you want to go?" As a fighter, you just see it in his eyes. If I go on the ice and I see that we're down by two goals and the other team has put one of their tough guys out there and I've been put out there, I know what's supposed to happen. And the other guy knows why I'm going out. There are other times when it's more spontaneous. But you've always got to be ready as a fighter. Things can turn on a dime pretty damn quickly.

I think most fighters don't love doing their job, but ultimately if that's what's going to keep them in the league, that's what they're going to do. There are a lot of guys in the NHL or in juniors who are willing combatants only because that's what they're told to do. Do they like doing it? Probably not, but whatever is going to take them to the next level, they're going to do it. But for me, because of the way I grew up and the things I had to fight for, I don't mind doing it at all, even though I know there are other elements to my game. If we play a team and they've got four or five guys who are willing combatants, then *Yeah, fuck, let's go.* There aren't a lot of teams that have players like me. I live and die for my teammates. They're my brothers. They're the reason why I'm there every day, ready to go to war and do battle. I want to be that person. Being able to change the momentum of the game or lift the guys up with a fight is rewarding. I get satisfaction from that.

I understand that you put your life at risk when you fight, but for me there's no fear. Once you start experiencing fear, that's when you know you're starting to go downhill. Every game I go into, I'm confident. Confidence is everything. It's unbelievable what the mind can do for you. If you start second-guessing yourself before you go into a fight, you're fucked right then and there. I've had a lot of guys, junior hockey guys, come through training camp and say, "Hey, you're not the biggest guy. Have you got any tips for me? I'm kind of a fighter. What have you got?" Guys ask who taught me how to fight: "In the off-season, what did you do . . . train like a boxer?" Fuck, no. I'm not that kind of fighter. I'm a hockey player. If I was a fighter, I'd fucking train for MMA or boxing. Fortunately, the way I grew up is what's carried me through my whole hockey career. I had to learn how to stick up for myself when I was fricking seven years old, so why wouldn't I do it now?

It's just like throwing a switch for me. Early in my career, I only knew how to throw rights. Today, I can throw with both hands. That was part of the process of learning how to fight. Now I'll go toe to toe with anyone. Obviously, with heavyweights it's a different story. I may take a beating and, when that happens, you mentally lose confidence. For a minute, I think, *Fuck, do I really want to keep doing this?* But my confidence always comes back.

Some guys in the dressing room are like, "Geez, how do you keep doing it?" I don't really know. I'm not a great teacher, but I give them one piece of advice: you have to go in believing you can win. Don't ever second-guess yourself. The other guy will know it; you'll know it. A lot of guys I fight, when I ask them to go and they're just like, "Aw, fuck . . .," and then they hesitate. I know right then I've got them. That's the biggest part of the game for fighters now: understanding your mental preparation.

What does it feel like to be in a hockey fight? You find out you have muscles you never knew you had before. And you're so in the zone. It's just me and the other guy. You know it's going to happen. You can see it in the guy's eyes. *Fuck, he wants to go.* You know you've got him beat mentally and that's half the battle. You know that just by looking in his eyes. But you still have to stay composed, because you're not going to win every fight. Some guy will catch you with a lucky shot, and that's part of the game, too. It's all about will, about fighting for dear life.

Everything else that's going on in the rink is blacked out during a fight. I have one goal at that moment, and that's to fricking pound the piss out of this meathead because either he asked me to go or he did something to my teammates. And when you're in that state of mind where you want to kill—there's an edge there and if you go over it, that's when you'll get hurt. There's a fine line between being in control and being out of control. So, as much as you want to pound the piss out of this guy, there's a lot of shit going through your mind. If you go over that fine line, that's when you get knocked out or you fucking blow your knee out. So, it has to be a controlled anger. And after the fight, it's all over. There's no retribution. But if need be, I'm willing to go again. If it happens, it happens.

The best part about being a fighter is the support you get in the dressing room. When the guys actually appreciate what you're doing for the team, it's more enjoyable. When you don't get that feedback, don't get that love from the boys, I think that's when you start losing interest. You'll come into the dressing room at the end of a period after you've had a fight and you can't even talk you're so exhausted—you're huffing and puffing. The guys will come up to you and just tap you with their sticks. They don't have to say anything. You know that's a sign of appreciation, their way of saying, *We know what it's like.* Of course, the fans love the fights. They love that part of the game, and it's great to give them what they want and hear the cheers. But for me, the most important part is what you feel in the dressing room. You have that euphoric feeling of being wanted. You feel that you're loved and appreciated for all of the shit you've gone through and put yourself through for the team. I did that for six years in Nashville, and that's what kept me there. If I hadn't done it, the fans wouldn't have loved me and maybe the coaches wouldn't have thought, *This is why we're keeping him here.*

The game evolves every year and things change. You've got to be able to skate and play and do all that other stuff as well. Over the last couple of years, I've gained more clarity about why fighting is part of the game and why I'm called upon to do it, rather than simply fighting in anger or to please the crowd because that's what they want to see.

When I was still partying a lot, there was no controlled anger for me. I was fucking all-in because of all the anger I had away from the rink. That was all coming out when I fought. I didn't care if the guy standing in front of me was a skill guy or a fighter. If I was fighting a skill guy, fuck him. That was his problem. Luckily, I didn't hurt myself too badly—knock on wood— before I straightened out my life and got sober.

I know the stories of guys like Derek Boogaard and Rick Rypien—fighters who had all kinds of problems that eventually cost them their lives. But I'm happy. My life is in control. If I was still partying, I'd be a miserable man. But it wouldn't be because of fighting.

TEN

*J*ordin scored only 4 goals in his first season with the Predators, and had 4 assists. But even while playing limited shifts in 70 games, he accumulated 130 penalty minutes, a pretty fair indication of the style of game he brought to the league. In the following season, the NHL locked out its players in a labour dispute and eventually cancelled the entire schedule. Because he was on a two-way entry-level contract, Jordin was sent down to the Milwaukee Admirals of the American Hockey League, the Predators' number-one farm team. While some of his teammates sat through an enforced year off, or travelled to Europe in search of playing opportunities, Jordin gained experience during a second full season of professional hockey. In the following season, 2005–2006, Jordin split the year between Nashville and Milwaukee. Then, in 2006–2007, he fully established himself as an NHL player. He wasn't the scorer he had been during his final two seasons in junior hockey, and he wasn't playing on the first line. But he settled into a comfortable role: the "energy *guy" who plays a handful of shifts in every game, lays on some hits, fights occasionally, and adds adrenalin to the mix. The fans in Nashville learned to look forward to those moments when Jordin jumped over the boards. They knew it meant guaranteed action. And they saw in him an undersized underdog with an exotic background, a guy who was fearless and who would do anything to help his team win. There were other stars on the Predators roster—and for a time, in 2007, the team was stacked with talent, including Peter Forsberg and Paul Kariya. But no Predator was more beloved than Jordin Tootoo. He was a fan favourite, he was a celebrity, and he was the toast of the town. For Jordin, it was a great time to be young, and well paid, and famous. There were benefits . . . and there were consequences.*

I think, for me, it was the easiest transition there could have been for a small-town kid going to the NHL. Nashville is not a big city. My travel to the rink and home wasn't that far. It was kind of a perfect scenario, rather than being in Toronto or Philadelphia, which are massive cities with so much temptation all over the place. Not that there wasn't any temptation in Nashville, as I found out. . . .

They loved my style of play in Nashville. That's what really grabbed the fans. They didn't grow up with the game, they didn't know much about it or about its history, so hockey is pure entertainment for them. All they knew was that the Predators were playing that night and Tootoo was in the lineup and he was going to fight for sure. They wanted that, and I knew it. I knew what the fans were looking for, and I gave it to them.

The next thing you know, I was a household name in Nashville. The team was happy with it because I was doing my job, doing everything that I was asked to do, and I was keeping the paying customers happy. By about halfway through my rookie season, it felt like everyone was talking about me. I might even have sensed a little jealousy from a few of my teammates regarding my popularity. They must have been thinking, *Fuck, this kid's new on the team. I've been here for four years, and he's getting all the attention. What the fuck?*

At first, I was really careful about what I did away from the rink. But when I started getting regular playing time with the Predators and knew that I had a guaranteed spot—knew that I wouldn't be sent down to the farm team in Milwaukee—I started cutting loose. I decided I could party it up a bit. When I first got to Nashville, I was underage in the States, where the drinking age is twenty-one, but I found a couple of buddies who owned a bar where all of the guys on the team would hang out in a back room and get lit up, and then drag a few broads out of there. Southern girls. I started going out more and meeting more and more broads. Being a bit of a local celebrity made it easy, and all of the temptation was there. In the places I went, people knew who I was. I could go downtown and walk the streets and no one would know me, because it was still just hockey in Tennessee. But there were places I knew I could go and meet some women, and know that I would get a guaranteed pickup. For me, that's what it was all about.

I was with a lot of women in Nashville. Lots. *Lots.* And by "lots" I mean . . . well, you know. I was a man-whore. I had steady girlfriends, but there's always someone hotter out there. I didn't want to be alone. I was living on my own, but girlfriends would stay with me. I had a couple of steady girlfriends who were always available, but when I was out, I would party. I feel badly for my girlfriends who had to put up with my bullshit and with me constantly lying. But I grew up lying. All I knew was lying.

I always told myself it wasn't the booze that killed me, it was the hunt. I'd go out and have dinner by myself, drink a couple glasses of wine. Then I'd call a couple of buddies, we'd go someplace, and the next thing you know, it was two o'clock in the morning. *Well, fuck, I've got practice at ten o'clock—I'd better get on the horn to find a fucking broad.* So, yeah, I fucked around a lot; I'm not going to lie about it. That was me trying to fill the void. Part of me wants to blame my brother for not being around, but that would just be me being selfish and blaming someone else. That would be a cop-out for me. That would be an easy excuse.

I did have one girlfriend in Nashville who you might have heard of. Her name is Kellie Pickler. She was on *American Idol* and has had a pretty successful singing career, but the truth is, when I met her I had no clue who she was. But by the time I met her, a lot of people in the Nashville country music scene knew who I was. It's a small town and I was in that loop. One day, at the condo building where I was living, the concierge said, "Hey, I've got a perfect match for you, Jordin. I know you bring a lot of women in here, but this one is going to be a good girl for you. Beautiful blonde. She's new in town. She's never been to a hockey game. We were talking about hockey today and I kind of threw your name out there, saying that one of the Predators players lives in this building—maybe he can get you a couple of tickets." *Boom. Done. Come and get the tickets.* I got Kellie passes to come to a game.

I knew in the back of my mind that this broad must be fucking hot so, of course, during the game I had to fight. I had to show her that this is what it was all about. I got into a scrap and I was kind of marked up after the game. After I got dressed, I went down to the family room, which is where the players meet their guests. I had no idea who this girl was or what she looked like, other than that she was a blonde and beautiful. I walked into the family room and all of the players' families were sitting around, and I didn't see anyone who matched that description. Then I looked toward a couch in the back of the room and I saw this stunning fucking blonde. That had to be her. She was the only one there.

"Is your name Kellie?"

"Yeah."

"I'm Jordin."

It went on from there. It was a Saturday night and we had Sunday off. Kellie was underage; I think she was nineteen or twenty years old then. And she wasn't really well known around town yet. So I took her to Tin Roof, a bar where all the players used to go. Of course, one thing led to another. We were getting all pissed up. The night ended. We both lived at The Enclave condominiums, so we took a cab home together. Nothing happened that night. I gave her a call the next day. We started hanging out. I showed her around town. I knew where the hot spots were. Three weeks went by and we decided we would start seeing each other. She basically moved into my place. We started having fun, and the rest is just details.

I even took her up to Rankin Inlet one summer, but it didn't go very well. People thought I was king shit, dating a famous country singer. But she wasn't welcomed very well by my family and friends, and I have to admit that I didn't make it easy for her. She was up there for four or five days and I partied hard for three of them and kind of left her alone with my folks. It wasn't good. She didn't eat. Not just our Inuit food—she didn't eat anything. I didn't know that, because I was fucking gooned for most of the time she was there. So when she got on the plane to fly south to Winnipeg, her blood sugar level was way out of whack. She ended up collapsing on the plane. I got a call from the Winnipeg police saying that they had Kellie, that they'd had to take her off the plane on a stretcher and put her in an ambulance. She almost died. She ended up in the hospital for two days and had to cancel some of her shows.

As the significant other, of course I should have been on the next plane to her. But, instead, I called my buddy Mike Young, who was in Winnipeg then, and asked him to babysit Kellie in the hospital so I could stay in Rankin Inlet and keep partying. Needless to say, when I returned to Nashville and saw her again, things started going downhill fast. It's probably the only time I'll ever be in *People* magazine. They did a story about us dating. And then they did another one about us breaking up—though they didn't get the real story, which for me was probably a good thing. Here's what happened: I got a new cellphone, and when I took off for practice one morning I left my old phone on the coffee table in my condo. You probably can guess where this is going.

After practice, I turned on my phone and there were, like, ten text messages. "Get your ass home we need to talk." "Where are you?" All that plus a whole bunch of missed calls.

I called Kellie right away and said, "What are you doing? You know I was in practice."

All she said was: "You need to get your ass home right now."

I could tell from the tone of her voice that it wasn't good, but I wasn't sure what I'd done wrong. I got home, opened the front door, and looked down the hallway toward the living room. On the coffee table, I could see a case of Bud Light—and as I got closer I could see that there were four beers missing. I asked Kellie what she was doing, drinking at 12:30 in the afternoon, but she wasn't interested in that conversation.

"You fucking sit right down here," she said. Then she pulled my old cellphone out of her pocket. "You have anything to say?"

"No," I said, "but it looks like I'm going to be here for a while, so I might as well crack a beer with you."

I knew what was coming. We went through that case of beer while I sat there and got an earful for a good two or three hours. She read out text message after text message.

"So, here's one from Wednesday, January 23, 12:05 am—that's the night the bus picked me up at midnight to go out on tour. . . . 'Hey, sexy. She's gone. The front door is open.'"

It was bad. Time for another beer.

We tried to work things out for a few months after that, but needless to say it didn't happen. I couldn't handle it anymore—or maybe she couldn't handle it. And then, later, she wrote a song about me. An angry song. It's called "Best Days of Your Life." There's a video that goes with it, where she's singing with Taylor Swift, and there's a guy in it who's supposed to look like me. At the end of the video, he gets hit by a bus.

Once he was established and had become comfortable as an NHL player in Nashville, Jordin's life off the ice began to look not much different from the life he'd lived in Brandon as a junior hockey star. There was always a place to go, always a party, always someone to buy him a drink and pat him on the back. But, now, there was another element to Jordin's drinking and carousing: the need to dull the painful memories of Terence's suicide, to avoid being alone with all of the unanswered questions about why it had happened and whether there was something he could have done to prevent it.

I had a group of drinking buddies on the Predators: Scottie Upshall, Chris Mason, David Legwand, Adam Hall, and Scott Hartnell. We were all the younger guys on the team and most of us were western Canadian boys. I can tell you, it was a good time—too good of a time.

Uppie is my boy. I met him way back at a tournament in Edmonton when we were thirteen or fourteen years old. We hit it off right away. He's a gem, I'll tell you. A real beauty. His family is originally from Newfoundland, but he grew up in Fort McMurray, Alberta, before it got so big and crazy. He's still got a little bit of a Newfoundland accent. As kids, we played together on a couple of Alberta Selects teams, and once went down and played in a tournament in Minnesota. What I remember most about it is that the only time I ever saw Uppie was at the rink. The rest of the time he was out golfing. I'm sure that when his hockey career is done he's going to be a pro golfer. He's got great skills.

Then we played against each other in junior—me in Brandon and him in Kamloops. Uppie was a great junior player. All I'll say about it is that he knew who ran his show; I fucking ran his show. He knew not to fuck around with me. And then Uppie got picked in the first round of the draft by Nashville. It's funny how everything worked out: I got drafted by the Predators, and then he got drafted by the Predators. I thought, *Shit, we just can't leave each other alone.*

We joke around a lot. I call him Scottie Too Hottie, the Devil Boy, which ought to give you a clue as to what he's like. The guy thinks he's the fucking hottest guy walking around. He's a good-looking guy and he carries himself in a certain way. He's someone who can talk to anybody at any time. He's a lot of fun—but I don't think a lot of other people have had as many good times with him as I have. He's also a guy who is there to listen and understand. He's a team guy first. I could see that right from the day we first met. He's a leader. He's a guy who wants to be counted on to make a difference and take that pressure on.

The best thing that happened in his career was probably when Uppie was traded from Nashville to Philadelphia in 2007. We were running pretty hard together and it was starting to show.

Word had started getting out. When he was traded, everyone came up to me and said, "Your buddy is gone; now what are you going to do?" I figured out what to do. (Now Uppie's an alternate captain with the Florida Panthers and enjoying life. I'm proud of where he's at.)

I was living on my own, with no curfew. My routine was that on the night before a game, I'd kill a couple of bottles of wine, feel good. I'd wake up the next day, do the morning skate, sleep all afternoon, play six shifts a game, get into a fight—it was easy, at least at first. And then as I became more established and more successful and the coaches started to rely on me more, I started playing more minutes. But my life away from the rink hadn't changed and it was killing me. I was playing ten or more minutes per game and by the ninth or tenth or eleventh minute I was thinking, *Holy fuck, I'm dead.* I couldn't perform to the best of my ability, and so I had to start taking advantage of my role as the enforcer. If I had been partying and I was dead on the ice and I knew I didn't have the legs, I'd get into a fight as fast as I could, just to get the five minutes off in the penalty box. I knew that if I scrapped a couple of times, the team would be happy and the fans would be happy and I wouldn't have to work as hard that night.

But I still partied. A Saturday night game, a day off on Sunday—*let's get after it, boys.* I was a weekend binge drinker. It wasn't like I'd wake up in the morning and need a drink. It's just that when I drank, I'd fucking drink like I was from the Far North—you know, that's in my blood. I could drink for two days straight, no problem. So I partied hard. All booze. I was never was into drugs or anything; booze was my drug. I'd fucking get after it on Saturday nights, all night, and just be a maniac. I wasn't a guy who was violent or anything, because I'd seen enough of that growing up. For me, drinking was entertainment. I was a happy drunk. But I would force people to drink with me, just like my dad does. If you're going to be around me, you're going to drink with me all fucking night. And I was happy to buy every round.

I was a very well-known guy in Nashville, and any time we went out and had a night off it was, like, fucking Jordin Tootoo and his buddies are here and the party's on. No one knew my teammates, and I always used that as an excuse when I was called into the coach's or general manager's office after a bender and they weren't. The team would get a call from someone saying, "Tootoo was in the bar all day Sunday drinking and watching football. Doesn't he work?" I wasn't going to throw my teammates under the bus; instead, I would take the heat and come out of the office believing that everything would be good—I'd fucking play great the next game and they'd forget all about it. That went on for a couple of years, and just about every weekend David Poile would get a call—and then Barry Trotz would call me into his office and ask me what the fuck was going on. But why was it always me?

It got to the point where Poile called me in and told me I needed to figure things out or else he'd put my name in headlines across North America, because the team would cut me or release me. I didn't believe him. I figured I was their fucking go-to guy and there was no way they'd do that. I had the same mentality as

Theo Fleury; I thought I was unstoppable. *You're going to cut me or trade me? Go ahead and try it and see what the fans say.*

Eventually, my teammates stopped hanging out with me as much, because they knew I would be going hard, every time out, and they didn't want to do that anymore. But I didn't see that. I just wondered why none of the boys wanted to go out with me, and then I found friends outside of hockey who were willing to go out any time I wanted, for as long as I wanted, and had nothing to lose.

After a game, the bars in Nashville would be ready for me. They'd figure, *The Predators won tonight, so Toots will be here around midnight. Let's get his corner ready.* In the early days I went to the popular places. But toward the end of my drinking days, I hung out in fucking dark places, little holes in the wall where I wouldn't be seen—or at least where I thought I wouldn't be seen. The truth is that a lot of people still knew I was going out, but in my mind I was out of sight in these little fucking holes in the wall.

On the ice, I was a scary guy in those days. I'm sure that the players on other teams hated me—and probably they still do—but now they at least understand that I'm a more controlled freak than I was then. Before, during practice, even my teammates didn't know what the fuck I was going to do. They'd be thinking, *Don't piss off Toots. He's not all that great today. He might go off.* I didn't see that part of myself and I let so many guys down. What a fucking shitty teammate I was.

Guys on my team would ask me, "You okay, Toots? Is everything okay at home?" All they had to do was look at me to know what kind of shape I was in. But I didn't think there was a problem. It was no big deal . . . whatever. But that's not what I saw in their eyes.

In those days, I got into a lot of fights just because I wanted to pound the piss out of somebody—out of anybody. There was a lot of shit going through my mind that came out in those fights. It's supposed to be a controlled anger when you fight, but when I was partying, there was no control. I was fucking all-in. All of the anger I had outside of the rink was coming out on the ice. I didn't care if there was a skill guy or a fighter standing in front of me. Fuck him. I just kept wrapping myself around booze and then went to the rink and let it all out. When you're using substances, they trick your mind. Something little may happen and, frick, you snap.

A bunch of times, I made pacts with my teammates. I stood up in private meetings with them and promised that I wasn't going to drink that month, or that I was going to quit drinking cold turkey. I'd tell them I was sorry that I had let them down, that I was going to change, that I wanted to quit drinking for them. They'd just sit there and listen and, you know, I'd feel good after telling them I'd quit. But I could see in their eyes that they were thinking, *Aw, fuck, Toots, here we go again. You're just bullshitting us again. You're going to fall off the wagon in a couple of weeks anyway, so let's not get our hopes up too high.*

And they were right.

By the beginning of the 2010–2011 season, things had gotten really bad. I was drinking twelve cans of beer on a Saturday night, and then fifteen, and then adding shots, and the next thing you knew, I was hung to the gills for two or three days afterwards. It was affecting my play, and everyone knew it. I needed someone to lay down the law, to tell me I couldn't do it anymore. Otherwise, I would have just kept on going, and really lost something that I love.

ELEVEN

On December 18, 2010, the Predators were beaten 6–1 by the Los Angeles Kings in front of a disappointed home crowd of 16,734 at what was then known as the Gaylord Center, now the Bridgestone Arena. The loss broke a five-game winning streak and it was the first time the high-flying Predators had lost in regulation time since November 28.

With three days off before their next game in Chicago, and with a busy schedule throughout the holiday season, the team held its Christmas party after that game. It would be a landmark day in Jordin's life, for reasons that had nothing to do with hockey.

My buddy Troy was down from Rankin Inlet for what turned out to be my last night of drinking. Troy and I have been pretty much blood brothers since almost our first day of life; we were born two days apart. It's kind of funny how it all went down. We were together the first time I tried booze as a kid, and he was the last person I partied with before I quit drinking.

That week we played on Saturday night and had Sunday off, which was always a recipe for hard drinking. Troy was going to be in town for a few more days, and so it was a green light for us to have at 'er. The first night was pretty close to an all-nighter. Troy's mom and girlfriend were staying at the condo and we came barging through the doors at four o'clock in the morning, all pissed up and causing a ruckus, waking everyone up.

But that wasn't the end of it.

The next day, the Tennessee Titans were playing at noon, so we got up and said, "Let's find some tailgate parties."

Troy's mom, who has always been there for us, was worried. She said, "Make sure you guys behave yourselves. I think you're kind of out of control."

Of course, we told her we were okay, even though we weren't. We went to the football game and that turned into an all-day drinking event. Then, in the evening, Garth Brooks was playing at the arena and we had a mandatory team function there; I had to show up. We went to the Gaylord Center and, of course, we were three sheets to the wind by then. We got to the concert and Troy and I were stumbling around looking like idiots. Then, after the concert, we decided to go out again. It was turning into almost a forty-eight–hour binge. Troy and I ended up going out downtown. He finally called his girlfriend to come and pick us up. She basically had to carry us into the taxi and get us home.

The next day I got up, went to practice, and played what

most hockey players call "guilty hockey"—where you work extra hard to try to show that you weren't really out the night before. After practice, David Poile called me into his office to explain a phone call he'd received the day before. I think what happened was that a few of the workers in the Gaylord Center saw me and told someone that Tootoo was out of control, and word got back to Poile.

I was still hung to the gills and I reeked of booze. I was thinking, *What the fuck did I do now?*—and I really didn't know. I tried to trace events back to Saturday night, but I had no clue. I had been so drunk I'd blacked out. Of course, the first thing I did was deny any wrongdoing. I said that it hadn't been me. I played the "popular" card. It had been a team party and of course I was singled out of the twenty guys that were having a good time, because people know who I am.

Poile had heard all of that too many times before, and he wasn't buying it anymore. He gave me an ultimatum. He said, "If you don't accept what we're offering you, we've got to let you go. You're damaging our team. You have to enter the NHLPA substance abuse program and go into rehab or we're going to cut you, and everyone will know why."

Right then and there, I decided I wasn't going to fight it anymore. I said, "Fuck, I'm done. Let's go."

I haven't had a drink since. Not one.

I didn't tell Troy what had happened, though he knew I was in some kind of trouble. I didn't tell a fucking soul. On December 20, I went to a facility in Nashville to have what they called an assessment. I told Troy that I had a meeting and had to leave for a few hours, but I didn't tell him where I was going. But I think he knew something was going down.

We played our next game on December 23 and I just went about my business without saying a thing. We played on December 26 in St. Louis. Nobody knew that I was going to get shipped out. I played on December 26 and kept my cool. I played, like, seventeen fucking minutes. On December 27, I had breakfast with Troy and his family, and then they went to the airport to fly home. That afternoon, I shipped out.

I didn't have a drink during that period. I didn't want to touch alcohol. It wasn't like, *I'm going to rehab, so I want to get trashed one last time.* I was done.

After my meeting with Poile, he had contacted the National Hockey League Players' Association, and they had taken care of the arrangements through their substance abuse program. My contact was a guy named Dan Cronin. They sent a chaperone to pick me up and make sure I didn't miss my flight. I was thinking I was going to be away for a month, so I'd better buy an iPad and download a bunch of movies and some games—stuff to keep me busy while I was at this facility. The chaperone took me to the Apple Store and said, "Get whatever you need, no problem." So I spent $2000 on stuff. "No problem," he said. "No problem." I had no idea where I was going until I got to the airport and the chaperone put me on a plane to Los Angeles.

The only people who knew what was going on were Poile and Trotz. Not even my family or teammates knew. The team held a press conference that afternoon in Nashville, but only after I'd jumped on the plane.

I went into the program with an open mind. I wasn't in denial. I didn't fight it. I knew it was time and that I had to do it, for me personally and to save my career.

While Jordin was on the plane to Los Angeles, the Predators' coach and general manager informed the other players that he had gone into rehab. Then the team sent out a short, vague press release that revealed no details about Jordin's treatment. "We offer Jordin the full support of his teammates, coaches and the organization," said David Poile. "There is no timetable for his return and we will have no further comment at this time." But now the story was out.

I landed at LAX and turned on my phone, and things were just nuts. I was all over the news and my mom was freaking out. So I made four phone calls: to my sister, to my parents, to Scottie Upshall, and to my cousin Victor Tootoo, who used to have an addiction problem but who has been sober for twenty years. I told my mom that I was going to get help and that I needed to figure out my life. She said, "Okay, hopefully everything works out and I guess we'll see you when you get back." Uppie and my sister supported me, and I knew that, inside, my parents were happy as hell that I was changing my life.

I hadn't really known my cousin Victor until I was in my teens because he was a heavy addict. We kind of got to know each other over time, and he'd seen all of my partying. I called him and told him I was going into rehab. He didn't believe me at first, because we always joked around. So, I had to say it again: "I'm going to rehab, I'm in fucking LA, I'm going to a facility."

Victor still didn't believe me. I had to say it again. And then he stopped talking, and didn't say a word for twenty seconds. That's when it finally sunk in, not because of what I had said but because he'd just read it on the television news ticker: *Jordin Tootoo Enters a Substance Abuse Program.* He said, "I'm so sorry for how I reacted. I'm really proud of you." Of course, he could relate to what I was going through.

A car was waiting for me at the airport. It was dark out, so I had no idea which part of Los Angeles we were going to. Finally, I arrived at this place in Malibu with big fucking doors—like a mansion—and I thought, *This is going to be all right.* It turned out it was a famous place called The Canyon. If you follow Hollywood gossip, you've probably heard of it. A lot of stars go there to dry out. It's one of the places they took Lindsay Lohan.

I walked in there and left my bags at the door—and suddenly my bags were gone. They go through all of your shit to make sure you don't have any paraphernalia or booze or drugs. They took away my iPad, my iPhone, all of my electronics. That fucker in Nashville knew I wasn't going to get that stuff in, that as soon as I got there they were going to take everything away. I spent two fucking grand for nothing.

By the time I walked into The Canyon, I'd been sober for a week, a week and a half, so it wasn't like I needed to go through detox. But I still had to go through a process where they monitor you for a week. I had arrived in the middle of the night, when everyone was sleeping. I got up the next day, walked into a room, and saw all of these fucked-up people sitting around. We were sitting in a circle and I was looking around and thinking, *Am I really like this? Do I look like these people? What the fuck is going on? These people are in here for hardcore shit: heroin, cocaine.* But I had to understand that I was one of those people, too; I couldn't separate myself from the other patients. We all had problems and we were all trying to fix them. I couldn't just sit there and think, *I'm not fucked up like them.* I was there to fix myself. And at the same time, I couldn't be worrying about the other guys and how fucked up they were and stressing about their problems. I was there to fix myself.

The surroundings at The Canyon may have been luxurious, but Jordin's first accommodations there were relatively spartan: a simple, dorm-style room with two single beds and a door that was locked from the outside every night. This was the detox phase of treatment, although because Jordin hadn't had a drink since that last night in Nashville, he wasn't experiencing any of the physical symptoms that often come with withdrawal. He felt relatively normal. For the first couple of nights, the second bed in his room remained empty. And then, he got a roommate.

The door came flying open and this fucking guy who was just blitzed walked in. The orderlies were yelling: "Jordin, Jordin, we may need your help here! We need you to help calm him down!" *Fuck, I'm a patient. I don't work for you guys. I'm just going to sit back and watch the show.* The guy came storming in and I didn't know who he was. All I was told was that he was a big-league baseball player. I guess I don't watch that much baseball, or maybe I would have recognized him.

The guy walked in and he was just fucking mangled. I was looking at him, thinking, *I know that look. I've been there.* It was actually kind of entertaining at that point. I had my back against the far wall. And then the guy noticed me and started giving me the fucking gears. I was thinking that things might be a little out of control. He was screaming: "This is fucking bullshit! What the fuck? I'm forty-some years old and I'm in fucking rehab. What a joke!" Remember, I was dead-cold sober. I wasn't on any detox pills. Nothing. And by then, they'd locked us in there together—just the two of us. He was yapping away, blitzed, and going on and on, screaming at me: "You fucking asshole. Who the fuck do you think you are?" I kept telling myself, *Just keep your cool, Jordin. Keep your cool.* But he kept going on.

Then he said, "I'm going to knock you out with my baseball bat. I can fucking swing a baseball bat pretty damn good."

Finally, I said to him, "You don't have your baseball bat here. You see these fucking fists? That's what I fucking work with. So you'd better fucking shut up now or I'll shut you up."

Then it turned into a "fuck you" match and the next thing I knew I had my fist cocked and this guy was going to get it. But I didn't want to cause any shit because I didn't want to be in here any longer than I had to.

Finally, the orderlies came back in and they gave him a couple of doses of something and he just conked out. A half-hour later, it sounded like there was a fricking volcano on the other side of the room. It was four o'clock in the morning and the guy's snoring was just unbelievable. I was looking for earplugs and then I started banging on the locked door, and nothing happened. No one came to my rescue. I didn't get much sleep that night.

The next day rolled around and my new roommate came to. As he started snapping out of it, we clicked right away—*you're an athlete, I'm an athlete.* It turned out he was a guy named Jeff Bagwell, who played for the Houston Astros. I guess he was a pretty big deal. We got to know each other and like each other, and after that it was a piece of fucking cake.

A few days later, Jordin completed the detox phase of his treatment and moved out of the room he shared with Bagwell. Now, the harder part of the process would begin. Sealed off, with no contact with the outside world—no phone, no television, no internet—he began the process of changing his life. The challenge wasn't just to stop drinking. Jordin had done that, at least temporarily. It was also to dig down and try to find the root cause of that drinking, which, for Jordin, meant embarking on a painful trip through his past— though, initially, he thought it was going to be easy.

They took me to a different part of the building where I had more freedom. A month seems like a long time, but it didn't feel that way because I knew I was there to work, so the time fucking flew by. The hardest part for me was leaving the game and not being in contact with anyone who I could relate to or talk about hockey with. Remember, this was December and January, right in the middle of the season.

It was a "step" program at The Canyon, an introduction to how your mind and body work with substance abuse. Every day, you have group meetings and then individual meetings with your therapist. You have a workbook. They ask you all of these questions and then you do your homework. At first, I was flying through the fucking workbook. In the first two days, I was halfway done and thinking, *Is this all there is to it?* Little did I know that the workbook is just a starting point in getting to know a bit about yourself and digging—really starting to dig into your roots.

It had been a while since I'd read books and written shit down, because I'd never had to do that. My reading and writing skills got a lot better, because I actually started thinking and doing my work.

Some people at The Canyon were only there because other people wanted them to be there, and that doesn't work. I made sure that I was doing what I had to do for myself. That meant looking deep inside to find out how I had got to this point—kind of like a timeline. There were a few chapters in that workbook that related to my childhood, my upbringing, and my parents' upbringing. At first, I was a little timid about spilling the beans. I had to decide whether I was going to tell them how I actually grew up, or just fucking blow it off and get through it. At the beginning, I thought I just wanted to get through it. I didn't want to deal with any in-depth situations because it would cause more problems with my family. I didn't want my therapist having to contact my parents and have questions for them. I didn't need that. I didn't need my parents involved, telling a different story about how they raised me.

So, at first, I wasn't going to tell anyone about my personal issues from my childhood. I was going to do what I had always done, except for the time I fought my dad: shut up and put up with it. Up in the north, you just keep that stuff inside. If someone has a grudge against your family member, you don't talk about it, even though you live in the same town and see each other every day.

I tried to keep things inside, but then I would keep going back to those couple of chapters about my childhood and, every day, I would write just a little bit more and it was like a fucking weight was being lifted off my shoulders. That started opening doors for me. It gave me a way to get rid of those inner demons. And, really, that's why I'm here today.

My therapists left it up to me. They said that any time I had an issue, we could talk about it. I wasn't a big talker, ever, but the Canyon is where I really started to understand that communication is healthy. Without communication, it's pretty hard to get anywhere.

At the beginning, I was trying to not think about those issues. I was just trying to get past them. But, finally, I realized I was there to fix myself. That was part of how I needed to heal. I needed to understand how I got to this point, to understand why my parents are the way they are, to understand why people are the way they are up north.

I tried to deal with my issues. If I hadn't, fuck, I'd probably still be drinking. And the truth is, I still have a lot of issues. But rehab is where I really started to mature as a person, where I started loving myself, and where I started understanding how I got to that point.

When I talked to my parents after I got out, they didn't really understand any of that, because that's just the way they are. So I had to take different routes in asking them certain questions, because they're constantly on the defensive. And then, at the end of the day, I told them I still loved them for who they are.

I also talked to my therapists a lot about Terence, and about what had happened to him. For me, that was a positive. I understood everything that he'd taught me as a kid. To watch him grow up and be a strong-willed person with the courage and determination to fight through anything—that was stuff I learned because I grew up beside him. This was a guy I looked up to every day. This was a guy who was the definition of hard work, persistence, and commitment. That's what I saw in him. He was a guy who, if I had to go to war or any of our buddies had to go to war, you'd want beside you. That was Terence. He wasn't the biggest guy but, boy, was he strong. And if times were tough, you could count on Terence to get through them.

And then the day came when he decided he'd had enough and he was gone. That was hard for me to process. It still is. Part of me was mad at him. No question about it. Why would he do this to me? Why would he leave everything for me to figure out? Why would he leave me to deal with all of this shit on my own? Why would he come to that point when so much in his life was happy then? Why would a guy with so much mental strength do this? There's nothing that burns inside me more than that—it burned then and it burns now. A guy who I counted on every day and the next thing I knew, he was gone. . . . I admit that, after it happened, I questioned my own purpose in life. What am I here for if he's not going to be here? Frick, there were times when I second-guessed my life and whether I wanted to keep living it. Terence was a guy I counted on daily. When you lose someone that important to you and you don't understand why, it's pretty tough to get over. I used alcohol and women to try to fill that void, to distract me, sometimes to black me out. In rehab, I started to understand that.

But when we talked about Terence in rehab, I realized that I had so much more in life to prove. I wanted to carry on Terence's legacy. I realized that, frick, I couldn't keep pounding my head against the wall, trying to figure out what I could have done to save him. I guess everyone has their breaking point. In the state of mind that he was in that night, he was well under the influence and he made a split-second decision. With suicide, you'll never really know why. But for a guy to go out like that is a little selfish. When you take your own life, you're being selfish.

Knowing the shit that he and I went through, it was like, frick, I could kind of understand. He didn't want to fricking deal with it anymore. I understand that a guy can only take so much. With everything that was going on in his life, being a role model for a lot of these young kids, it was way too much for him to have to deal with. But I can't blame anyone other than Terence for him taking his own life. You can't put the blame on anyone else. You go through life experiencing shit that you don't want to experience, but in the end it was up to him. And I guess his time was up.

It might seem strange to some people, but even though it was painful, I enjoyed talking about Terence in rehab and I still enjoy talking about him—his presence is always around me. Despite what happened, thinking about him always makes me smile. And when other people talk about him, it actually helps me. He was like my soulmate. And now I'm plugging away in his memory.

So, that's part of what I did during my thirty days in rehab. I just put my head down and did all my work. The process isn't over. To this day, I'm still working on myself. We all have our own ways of dealing with things. In the past, I had trouble communicating. But now I'm open and I'm not so afraid to talk.

TWELVE

When Jordin was released from The Canyon, he immediately flew back to Nashville to join the Predators. On January 31, he participated in his first practice and spoke to the media for the first time since leaving for rehab. "The support I've gotten from my teammates, my family, the fans of Nashville, it has been unbelievable," he said. "Without their support, I probably couldn't have done it. I think the bottom line is that it's something I needed to do and, at the same time, I'm just happy to be back and thankful. . . . I'm just going to take it one day at a time. Right now, I'm just living in the moment and enjoying every bit of it. I can't tell you how far down I went. I'm just going to live in the moment right now."

The Predators' general manager and coach spoke as well. "Nobody's perfect," David Poile said. "We all have different issues in our life. I think that it just reached a situation where he was becoming more difficult and obviously a distraction to others in our *organization. The point is, and this is the most important point, Jordin got it and Jordin did it and he knows he's better off for it today."*

"He is dealing with it the right way and he's manning up and that's what you're proud of," Barry Trotz said. "He's manning up and taking responsibility and that's the first step for success. . . . As soon as the doctors give us the word, he'll be ready to go. His first focus is on getting order in his life and we support him 100 percent and then the hockey thing will come. He's working towards that."

After I got out of rehab, everywhere I'd go in Nashville, people knew my story, but luckily I didn't have to lock myself away. They understood my situation. And the support that I got from the hockey world and from home was just unbelievable. When you're in rehab, you can't receive any mail or anything and you're not allowed to talk about the outside world. But my therapist at The Canyon told me that they were getting fucking stacks of mail for me when I was there. It made me feel good to realize how many people were behind me and how many people cared about me. You don't realize that until something hits you hard.

There is a protocol you have to follow with the NHL/ NHLPA substance abuse program. Once you get out of rehab, they want to make sure that your life away from work is stable and grounded before you return to hockey. I stayed in Nashville when the team went on the road, and I had a mentor who had been through the program and who worked with me. He was a local guy who was in AA and had been sober for twenty-five or thirty years. I had to kind of shadow him. When you get out of rehab, there is definitely a lot of temptation. He helped to guide me onto the right track. We talked a lot about the people you talk to, the people you used to hang out with. I actually found the process really interesting. It was a bit like doing homework in high school. You jot down the names of the people in the crowd you hung out with and then try to figure out who your real friends are. There were some people who were my friends outside of my extracurricular activities—so, outside of my drinking and partying. And there were others who I realized were only hanging out with me because I was a public figure. They were popularity-seekers. They wanted to be around me only because they wanted to be in the public eye. They wanted to be noticed. At the time, I thought that those types of people were my friends, but after making those lists and having those conversations with my mentor, I started to realize that wasn't true. If I ever had a question, he was only a phone call away, and we went to AA meetings together three times a week.

The meetings were good for me. At first, I could relate to a lot of the experiences people shared, how their drinking controlled their lives. But eventually it got to a point where I felt like all of the negative energy was actually starting to drag me down. Hearing how shitty these people's lives were and how drinking had ruined their families and their work lives. I couldn't really relate to that. I still had a job—and it was a great job—and I still had a family that loved me.

There wasn't really a point in the process when I was told that I didn't need to go to AA anymore. They just kind of forgot about it, and I stopped going because I didn't really need it to stay sober. Everyone takes a different path. A lot of people swear by AA, and good for them. But everyone has a different route. For me, it was about relying on my family and my close friends—my true friends, not the hangers-on. It wasn't about going to meetings.

Even with that support, in a lot of ways I was on my own. I had to look at my life as a sober person, really for the first time since I was a kid. Things definitely looked different. There was clarity about why people acted the way they did, and why I acted the way I did. And then there was the process of taking responsibility for what I had done. I had to acknowledge all of the people I hurt during my years of partying. When you're in a state of mind where you don't know what's going on, you hurt people. I was never a physical person off the ice, so it wasn't like that, but I would put people down verbally when I was drinking. I didn't think all of the drama that I caused was a big deal when it was happening. But now that I was sober, I started to think about how I didn't make time for my family and friends when they visited, because the only thing on my mind was going out and partying.

The process of apologizing to all of the people I hurt took almost two full years. Some of them I knew, and some of them I hardly remembered. Random people would come up to me and say, "I'm proud of you for turning your life around, but do you remember when you did this to me?" I might have met this one person one time when I was blitzed out of my mind and not have a clue who they were, but I had to accept that I had done what they told me and take full responsibility for it. All I could do was say I was sorry, and if they chose not to accept my apology, that was up to them. But there were a lot of them. I kept thinking, *Holy shit, I never realized how many people I affected with my drinking.* For a while it felt like all I was doing was apologizing and apologizing. Was I really that bad of a drunk? I guess I was.

The toughest part was dealing with the people I knew and really cared about—my family and friends—and starting to understand what I had put them through. These were the people who I grew up with, who had been around me for my whole life, and who had distanced themselves from me because of my actions. I didn't understand why when they did it, but once I sobered up I had a better understanding, and it was a tough pill to swallow. I couldn't imagine my best friends having to deal with me. So, I took full responsibility. It was hard, but it was a process I had to go through.

I made a list and started working my way through it—all of the people who had stuck by me since childhood, who had always had my back. I thought about the shit that I had put them through and the pain—and not only them, but their spouses and their families, too. I used to go home to Rankin Inlet for a month in the summer and I would just expect them to hang out with me and drink with me. And if their wives or girlfriends objected, I would say, "Tell them to fuck off." How could they not understand? I was only home for a month; it was my time to party. After talking to those friends and talking to their wives and girlfriends, I started to realize how much uproar I had caused in their lives. I think a lot of those families dreaded me coming home because they knew it would be a shit show for a month.

When I went back to Rankin Inlet at the end of the 2010–2011 season, I made a point of visiting everybody and telling them about my whole experience, and admitting what I had done wrong. I needed them to understand why I was like that—and pretty much everyone did. They all forgave me. That's a testament to who your real friends are. Your real friends are the people who can forgive you when you fuck up.

I think my parents spent that time hoping that I wouldn't get off track. I would phone them before I went to bed at night, just to give them a sense of peace so they knew I wasn't out. I don't know if they had doubts about me pulling through, or if that was just their way of showing love and letting me know they respected my decision to get sober. Either way, it was always nice to hear their voices and to be able to let them know that everything was okay. At that point, they were trying to stay sober themselves, so we were kind of helping each other out.

BACK IN NASHVILLE, the biggest challenge was filling time and getting my life straightened out while I was waiting to get the green light to play hockey again. Some of my buddies came down to hang out and support me. One of them was my cousin Victor Tootoo, the guy I called just before I went into rehab. He came down from Iqaluit and helped me through the process. He understood because he had been through it twenty years earlier and had stayed sober ever since.

At least people in Nashville knew I had been to rehab, because it was in the news. I can't imagine what it must be like for a regular person coming out of rehab after living that kind of life for thirty or forty years and trying to change. Everyone around you would constantly be offering you drinks and expecting you to be what you used to be. I know that was the biggest thing my cousin Victor had to face. He was a big druggie and alcoholic, but no one knew that he went to rehab and cleaned himself up. So it took five or six years for everyone to understand that he was sober.

For me, it was different. My situation was public knowledge. When I came back from rehab, my teammates, the hockey community, and the city of Nashville all knew where I'd been, and they were all so supportive. Any time I went out and met people, they knew. I went to restaurants where I used to hang out when I was drinking and they'd say, "Jordin, do you want a glass of water? Do you want a Coke?" Whereas before they would have asked me what bottle of wine I wanted. So, that kind of thing made it a lot easier for me.

That being said, there was always that one asshole who wanted to be the person who could tell everyone that he saw Jordin drink and that he's fallen off the wagon. But the people who I was with and who I trusted always had my back.

It took about a year or a year and a half until it became completely natural, until I could go out to clubs and the same bartenders who used to serve me a glass of wine just handed me a water or a pop instead. It actually got to a point where it was kind of funny.

To be honest, I was never really tempted to start drinking again. I knew I was done with it. Booze has been right in front of my face since I quit, but it's never come to the point where I've wanted to drink. For me, it is all about living one day at a time and staying sober one day at a time. You can't tell yourself that you want to be sober for, say, three years and mark it down the calendar day by day, though I know that works for some people. For me, it's not like that. I guess everyone deals with their sobriety differently.

Because I'm in the public eye and part of my job is making appearances and going to events, I had to deal with some different challenges. When I first got out of rehab, we had team functions, and it was suggested that I shouldn't go. I understood why. They didn't want to put me in an awkward situation. But as time went on, I wanted everyone to understand that it was my choice not to drink. I made that point to everyone I was around: *Don't feel bad if you grab a drink. If I feel uncomfortable, I'll leave.* Eventually, everyone understood where I was coming from and I felt free to be myself.

The other challenge for me was to separate drinking from playing hockey. I always believed it was the norm, that one was connected to the other. Being a hockey player meant that you drank, and when you got the green light—no game or practice tomorrow—you'd go hard every time. Now that I look back at it, I understand that our job was to make sure we were at the top of our game every day. And I didn't give myself that opportunity. I didn't give myself the chance to be the best every day because of my addiction. Not that I was the only one. I've seen a lot of guys questioned by coaches or management over the years, asking them if everything is okay, because they know that they're going hard. It's kind of funny now. When I show up at the rink and guys are hung over and complaining about how terrible they feel, I think to myself, *I sure don't miss those days at all.* You hear them talking, saying that they feel like shit, wondering why they drank so much. Then they look at me and say, "You must feel great." Hopefully, they'll understand one day.

Of course, I didn't limit my drinking to my hockey friends and it's not like hockey caused my problems. It was me who took it to the next level. If the bar closed at two o'clock and I wasn't done, I'd be looking for the after-party. By the end of most nights, I wasn't drinking with hockey players, but I always knew that those other people would be around at the end of the night, because they knew that Tootoo was going to have booze at his house and everyone was welcome. For me, it was more about having the people around to keep me occupied and make time pass; looking back, I realize that it was more about that than about the drinking. I didn't care who came over as long as people were there and I wasn't alone. I'm sure things were stolen from my house without me knowing it, but I didn't care. I just wanted the company.

In those first weeks after I got sober, that was an adjustment. The crowd was gone, and at the end of the night I was alone. Thank God for Ambien, because there were times when I would be lying in bed at ten o'clock on a Saturday night, restless and wondering what I should do. I'd pop an Ambien, knowing that it would put me out and get me through to the next morning, get me through until tomorrow.

WHEN I GOT BACK on the ice after rehab, I noticed a huge difference. I felt amazing every day. And I had a new clarity and understanding of the game, plus a new recognition that when I was younger, and I was drinking, I just did what I had to do to stay on the team. I didn't think about the game much. I just did my job, rather than try to expand my game. Having conversations about the subtleties of the game with my teammates . . . that had just never crossed my mind before. I had been doing my job and that was good enough.

But now I had a better understanding of what I brought to the team, what kind of player I was, what it really meant to be a teammate. Mentally, I was a different player, and you could see it in my game. The coaches noticed that I could see the ice better, that I was making solid, smart plays. My confidence built up and built up. And having my legs every day was a big change. It was like, *Wow, I didn't realize I could play like this for this long.* It was as if there had been a cloud over me, and when I smartened up it was as if that cloud lifted away. I felt better about myself, and I knew that my teammates had more respect for me. Before I quit drinking, they were constantly saving my ass, whether they wanted to or not. If the coach asked a question about me and what I'd been doing off the ice, they covered for me. They covered for me on the ice when I was hung over. Now I could prove myself with my actions. Nothing had to be hidden. You could just see in their eyes that they felt differently about me, that they knew Toots was healthy now, they didn't have to make up stories to protect me, they didn't have to worry about what kind of mood I was in, and about whether I'd go off on them. The truth is, it was great not having to walk that tightrope anymore.

The NHLPA doctors had a meeting with my teammates when I first got back, just to brief everyone on the process I'd been through. And then a doctor looked at me and said, "Toots, do you have anything to say to your teammates?" I said, "No. I've said enough. I'm just going to go back to work." I think that was a relief to them, because they knew that I wasn't going to fucking bullshit them anymore. I didn't want to say something and not follow through—I just wanted to show by example. I wanted to be judged on what I did, not on what I said.

On February 19, the Predators took on the Phoenix Coyotes at home, which the doctors had decided would be Jordin's first game back. He played for a little over ten minutes, and didn't score a goal, record an assist, or get into a fight. But everyone on the team, everyone in the building, understood that was beside the point.

After I got out of rehab, the NHLPA doctors and our team doctors would talk to me every week and ask me how I was doing. They were trying to decide when my life was under control enough that it would be okay for me to get back into a game. Eventually, everything just fell into place, and they told me that the Phoenix game on February 19 would be my first game back. I had a couple of weeks to get ready for it.

It was nerve-racking counting down the days. I just tried to stay focused on maintaining my health. It was a daily thing, keeping in contact with the doctors. They asked me if I was hanging out with my old friends, if I was finding new ways to keep myself busy, if I was eating at home or going to restaurants. Stuff like that.

I wanted the process to be a lot quicker because I wanted to play right away, but I knew that the more I pressed to come back, the longer they would keep me out. So, I just kept my feelings hush-hush within myself.

The whole day leading up to the game, everyone was so happy. The Nashville fans had been watching me for five or six years and they had really missed the element that I brought to the game. I remember, in warm-ups, there were signs out in the crowd and people cheering me on. When I took my first step out on the ice, I got a standing ovation that lasted for five minutes. The crowd just went apeshit. That's when the emotion really hit me.

We were playing the Coyotes, and I remember their players getting up on the bench and tapping their sticks on the boards. It was one of those days that you wish would just keep going on. There were a lot of emotions. That night, it felt like the whole city of Nashville embraced me.

I've never come close to drinking again. I mean, frick, there are times when it's been tough, but I have great resources and people I can call and count on and talk to. When I need them, there are a lot of people around who help keep me grounded.

THIRTEEN

Coming through rehab, rejoining the Predators, and returning to the National Hockey League, sober, were all significant milestones in Jordin's life. And there would be one more around the same time, the unexpected continuation of a story that began a long time before.

I've said a lot here about women . . . girls . . . broads, and some of it hasn't been pretty. If I have offended anyone, I'm sorry about that. But now I want to tell you about Jennifer Salvaggio.

I met Jen way back when I was playing junior hockey with the Brandon Wheat Kings. I was making an appearance at a kids' hockey tournament on a Sunday afternoon—the usual stuff: show up at a local rink, sign a few autographs, and talk to the fans. I was nineteen years old at the time. When I got there, I saw this lovely lady helping to set up the booth. Of course, when I see a pretty girl I have tunnel vision. The only thing I'm thinking is: *How can I get this broad?* So we had a little chat. I asked her what she was studying in university. How was school going? What did she like to do? Well, she said, phys ed, science, and social studies. What? That's high school stuff. That's when she told me she was only fifteen years old. Holy shit, I got that one wrong! But we still exchanged numbers and just kind of kept in contact.

Jen is originally from Vancouver. Her family bought a business in Brandon when she was a kid and she and her parents, Cal and Anna, moved there when she was ten years old. She spent her high school years there. Her dad is a machinist and her family is old-school Italian.

After that first meeting, Jen and I went on a few dates before my season ended. I invited her to games and we started talking more. She turned sixteen that May. I figured she was old enough at that point. At first her parents wondered, *Who the hell is this Tootoo guy?* They weren't into sports all that much, and hockey definitely wasn't their game. When I first started coming around, they didn't know who I was or what I did. But then I met them a few times and they came around on the idea of Jen dating me.

By the end of the season, I would be out in bars, late at night, and at closing time I would call Jen to come pick me up and drive me home. She didn't even have a driver's licence. I would give her the keys to my vehicle and she'd pick me up and bring me back to her place. It didn't really register with me that it might not be a good idea to show up there at two or three or four o'clock in the morning after I was done partying. I admit that I was selfish. I didn't give two shits about what people thought. I was on my own schedule. Jen's parents had good reason to wonder, *Who does this kid think he is?* But Anna, Jen's mom, was the soft-hearted one. For some reason she had patience with me. She greeted me and always made sure there was food in front of me, even if I was pissed drunk. She'd always say, "You're a hockey player, you burn a lot of calories, I want to make sure you're fed." Anna always had a smile on her face, even at four o'clock in the morning. I called her my Mama Bear. And thank God I had Anna around to make me dinner, because I don't think Jen really knew how to cook anything at that age. Then, after I finished eating, I'd go down to the basement and pass out and Jen would go upstairs and sleep next to her parents' room.

Jen and I kept in contact through that whole summer. She even asked me to take her to her high school prom, which wouldn't happen until the following year. At the end of that summer, I moved to Nashville. Obviously, her parents weren't going to let her follow me there at sixteen years old, so we tried the long-distance thing. I played that year in Nashville, we kept in touch, and I told her, *Yeah, we're dating, we're together.* But, meanwhile, I was running around with all kinds of other broads. So that didn't really work out.

However, I returned to Brandon in June 2005 for the prom. By then, I'd spent some of my NHL money on a Dodge Viper—a hot, expensive sports car—and I drove Jennifer to the prom in that. There I was, a twenty-two-year-old NHL player, back in high school for a night.

At that time, Jen was going through some personal issues. She'd got caught up with the wrong crowd. I didn't need that in my life—having to deal with the people she was hanging out with, and having them associated with my name—so I distanced myself from her. Eventually, her parents kind of kicked her out of the house, so she moved in with her cousins in Vancouver. Every time I played there with the Predators, we'd hook up and hang out and enjoy each other's company . . . and then away I went until the next time. We'd talk on the phone every other month or so.

Every time we saw each other, it was a big piss-up. That's all she knew about me. Every time we were together, I got tanked and she partied right along with me. Then she just sort of went off the deep end. I didn't want anything to do with her if she was going to be hanging out with the wrong crowd. She was spending time with people who were associated with nasty things—drugs and all that stuff. I was never a drug guy. I was never into that. So I didn't contact her or talk to her for a good five years. I just cut off all communication. With my hockey career going well, I couldn't be associated with those kinds of people. I didn't even think about her. I had other girls and I moved on.

Five years went by, and by then I'd gone into rehab. I had been cut off from outside communication when I was in there, so the minute I got out I checked all of my messages. Somehow, Jen had got my number. It was the first time I had heard from her in five years. She left me a message that said, "Hey, we're thinking about you. My family is praying for you." After I returned to the team, the Predators were going to play in Vancouver the following month, so I called her up and asked her if she'd like to have dinner and talk about what was going on in my life.

At first, she was hesitant. She knew me, for better or worse, and she didn't think the rehab was going to work out. She thought I was just trying to crawl back into her life with my charm. By that time, Jen had turned her life around, too. Before, she had worked in the bar industry in Vancouver, but she'd got out of that scene and that crowd and was working with her family in a bakery owned by her cousin.

Jen told at least one of her relatives that there was no way she was going to meet with me. But she must have changed her mind, because we got together in Vancouver for dinner, and it lasted four hours. She probably said four words the whole time, while I talked and talked about everything I'd been through. The team was going to be in Vancouver for four days. At the end of dinner, I asked her if she wanted to hang out again the next day. She said, "Yeah, maybe. I'll let you know." That was as far as she'd go. But as soon as she got home, she called me and said she'd really like to hang out again. So we did, and she ended up staying the night with me but we didn't do anything. And, for me, that was fine because I wanted to repair our relationship. I had put her through a lot. There were a lot of things I needed to fix. I spent the rest of my time in Vancouver trying to prove to her that our relationship wasn't just about the intimate part. She was fucking blown away that I didn't even kiss her. We watched a movie and then both went to sleep in the same bed.

The next month, the Predators were back in Vancouver for the playoffs. You know how they say everything happens for a reason? I remember that when we found out we were playing the Canucks in the playoffs, the first thing I thought was that there couldn't be any more perfect timing to rekindle my relationship with Jen. I remember flying in to Vancouver and calling her. We had a game on Monday and a game on Thursday. I told her that I was going to make sure I found time to see her. She tried to talk me out of it, because it was the playoffs, the most important part of the season. She said, "You shouldn't be worrying about us. We have all summer to figure something out." I was thinking, *Okay, Jen, I hear you. But deep down in my heart, if I feel that it's right, I'm going to see you no matter what.*

It was crazy in Vancouver during that series. The playoff atmosphere was unbelievable. The intensity. The emotions. Everything is magnified. I couldn't walk down Robson Street without people recognizing me, so away from the rink I just stayed indoors. And that kind of worked in my favour, because I had a better chance of spending time with Jen by not being out and about. Jen stayed with me in the hotel the entire time, and still nothing sexual happened. She was waiting for me to try to make a move, but I didn't.

The Predators were the underdogs in that series. I remember that after going down 3–1, we won game five in overtime, and I was thinking, *Geez, we have a chance.* It gave us life. And you could feel the tension in the building in Vancouver. The fans were thinking, *Oh shit, we've got a series now.* I thought that was going to be a turning point, but it didn't turn out that way. We lost game six back in Nashville, which was really disappointing. But the time I got to spend with Jen made up for it.

That summer, I was living at my place in Kelowna and Jen commuted back and forth every weekend to visit me. That's when I told her that I wanted her to be my one and only. She wasn't quite ready to commit to that yet. She knew I was going back to Nashville, and we had tried the long-distance relationship before and it hadn't worked out. But she agreed to at least play the relationship out for the rest of the summer.

One day that summer, I was visiting with her parents. They still liked me a lot. I was having coffee with Jen's dad one evening after dinner and I said to him, "What would you think of your daughter moving to Nashville?" Remember, they're a strict, old-school Italian family, so I wasn't sure he was going to like the idea. But he said, "You know what, Jordin? Jen is a grown woman. It's up to her to make that decision. And whatever decision she makes, I'll support her." They knew what she had gone through in the past and her relationships with other guys—and like any parents they wanted to know she was in good hands. And they knew I had turned my life around.

That night, I asked Jen what she thought about moving to Nashville. She laughed. "That would be a huge decision for me—but good luck running that one by my parents." Then I told her I had already spoken to her dad, and her reluctance seemed to melt away. And that was that. She moved to Nashville, and for a while life was good.

But five or six months in, Jen wasn't happy. The lifestyle associated with being a hockey wife or girlfriend is obviously different than in your average relationship. It was good for the first little while, because there was a lot of excitement and there were a lot of new things to do. And then it got old. She wondered what she was doing there. She didn't have any purpose in Nashville. She had worked all her life, but she couldn't work in the States because she was Canadian. She had been independent since she was a teenager, but now she had to depend on someone else to live. I suggested that maybe she needed to go home for a while and think about what she wanted to do. I knew she would come back. She flew to Vancouver, spent a week there and kind of got refreshed, and then came back to Nashville. It's been fine and dandy ever since.

Because of her past experiences and the kind of people she hung out with, she needed comfort—someone who would look after her as a person, care for her, and love her. And I was that person. I wasn't interested in any other broads. I was done with that. That part of my life was over. But it took some time to gain that trust. She kept wondering if I'd really changed. It didn't help that when we would go out for dinner in Nashville, two or three broads would come up to me—ignoring her—and say, "Jordin, we don't see you anymore. How come you don't hang out?" It took a while before that stopped happening.

I'm not a guy who says more than he has to. But I can't talk about Jen without acknowledging how lucky I am to have her. I guess everybody wants to be loved for who they really are and I know deep down that she accepts me that way. Not only that, she is the most beautiful lady I've ever seen. She is beautiful from the inside out, and that's what I admire about her. She would go out of her way to help anyone. And she's got the heart of a lion.

I may get paid to get in people's faces on the ice and do some pretty tough jobs, but off the ice I've always been the kind of guy who sort of goes with the flow. Over the years, people have taken advantage of that. But Jen has never been afraid to ask the tough questions and get the facts straight. She's made me more like that. And it's a pretty great feeling to have someone like that looking out for you too.

I think Jen and I understand each other. She has known me from my past and I have known her from hers. You mature as a person and you start to understand what really matters to you and when someone is on the same page as you. We've been through a lot of ups and downs, but at the end of the day it's about having respect for each other and being honest, and knowing that the person will be by your side no matter what happens.

For my parents, it's been a little hard to let their youngest go. They met Jen when we first started dating. With me being so young then, they weren't expecting much from our relationship. With all of my other girlfriends, my mom knew they were just flings. But when Jen came back into my life and stayed, she had to deal with my mom—and moms are moms. I guess from a mother's perspective, any time a woman comes into your son's life and takes that special position in his life away from you, there's going to be a bit of tension between you and the bride-to-be. I love my mom to death, but at the same time she has to understand that Jen is in my life and we're going to start our own family together. I'm a grown-ass man. I'm not a baby anymore, and I know that loving Jennifer doesn't mean I love my mother any less.

On July 19, 2014, Jordin Tootoo and Jennifer Salvaggio were married in Vancouver, British Columbia.

FOURTEEN

On August 31, 2011, the hockey world was shocked to learn that Wade Belak, who had recently retired after spending most of fourteen seasons playing in the National Hockey League for five different teams, had been found dead of an apparent suicide in a Toronto hotel room. It was the third troubling death of a hockey fighter in a few short months, following Derek Boogaard's drug overdose and Rick Rypien's suicide. For Jordin, Belak's death hit particularly close to home.

I met Wade late in 2008 when the Predators picked him up from Florida in a trade. He became my new road roommate. Most fans know him from the seasons he played with the Toronto Maple Leafs, and everyone in the hockey world knew who he was and the kind of player he was. But I got to know him personally, because we wound up rooming together for the better part of a year. It turned out we had a lot in common. We'd faced a lot of the same obstacles throughout our hockey careers, so we could really relate to each other. He was a Saskatchewan boy, a small-town boy from North Battleford. And he'd had to fight his way into the NHL. It wasn't long before he became almost like a brother to me—kind of like Jim McKenzie had been when I first arrived in Nashville. Wade wasn't the most skilled player on the ice, but when it came down to sticking up for his teammates, there was no one better. It was an honour just to play with him, to be at his side and learn the ropes from him and see the game through a fighter's mind. I was a fighter, too, but Wade was a true heavyweight.

He was always happy. He smiled all the time. Really, Wade seemed like the happiest guy around. And he was a real jokester. He played a lot of random jokes on me. I was okay with that because of how much I respected him. Outside of a hockey fight, he would never do harm to anyone. And he had a great presence; he just lit up a room. I'll always remember one of the crazy things we used to do. The night before a game, we'd both take an Ambien at the same time to help us get some sleep. But then we'd put $500 on the nightstand. Whoever stayed up the longest got to keep the money.

Wade would always tell me: "Toots, play your game. You're a good player. You can score goals. All of that other crap that I have to do . . . don't worry about that. I'll take care of it. I've got your back." When someone tells you that, someone like Wade or Jim McKenzie who has the power to bust people up, it makes you feel comfortable. Those guys were the toughest guys in the NHL. Having them by my side was an amazing feeling. I have been fortunate to play alongside guys who are heavyweights and who have fought through battles like I have.

Let me give you an example of what I'm talking about. There was a game with the Washington Capitals when they had Donald Brashear on their team. I laid Brashear out in the corner. Part of my game is being physical; it was a clear shot, and I took Brashear out. Of course, he wasn't happy about it. He got up and started tapping me on the back of my legs, trying to get me to fight. *Fuck,* I was thinking, *are you kidding me?* I'm a brave enough guy, but that was a bit of a mismatch. The next thing I knew, Wade came storming over and he actually knocked Brashear out with one punch. There's a clip of it on YouTube, I believe. Right after that, on the next shift, I went at it with a guy named Matt Bradley, who was actually bigger than Brashear, and busted him up pretty good. I did my duty. That one's on YouTube as well.

I couldn't believe it when I heard that Wade had committed suicide in 2011. Really, I still can't believe it. I don't know all of the details. The Wade I knew enjoyed every day of his life. He was a family guy. He had a wife and two kids. He was one of the best teammates I ever had. And he seemed happy being retired from hockey, enjoying every day to its fullest. He was doing the TV show *Battle of the Blades.* It seemed like he had everything going for him. It just goes to show you that life is lived day by day and hour by hour. You never know what will happen.

Because of what my family had been through after Terence died, I knew how it felt to have a loved one commit suicide, but I still couldn't imagine how his family dealt with it. I passed on my condolences and let them know that I understood what they were going through, and that we were all in this together. Any time you lose a brother or a friend, it's like life kicks you right in the balls. The test is how you react to it. Are you going to fold and crumble and let it beat you, or get up and live to fight another day? You're going to experience feelings you could never imagine in your worst dreams. But you have to pick yourself back up. No one is going to do it for you. Sometimes, though, it takes time.

Following his strong play during the Predators' playoff run in the spring of 2011, Jordin entered the 2011–2012 season feeling more confident than ever, and it showed on the ice. His game had evolved. He was still willing to drop the gloves when necessary, but his penalty minutes fell off significantly, while on offence he was starting to make more of a contribution than at any time during his NHL career. By season's end, he'd finish with 6 goals and 24 assists in 77 games, numbers that when combined with his physical presence and his high-energy style made him the kind of player that every NHL general manager covets. It was also the final year of his contract with the Predators, and because of his years of service, he would have the option of becoming an unrestricted free agent for the first time in his career, able to sell his services to the highest bidder. Nashville had been his only home in professional hockey, and Barry Trotz, who'd stood by Jordin during the tough times and helped him develop his game, had been his only coach. Jordin loved the city, and loved the fans, and they loved him back. When he'd returned from rehab, they had supported him. And every time he stepped on the ice, he could hear that ripple of excitement in the crowd, anticipating another Tootoo moment. But professional hockey is a business, careers are short, and when the opportunity arrives for a player to sign a life-changing contract, there's little room for sentiment.

David Poile, the Predators' general manager, offered me a contract extension in December 2011, but I turned it down. It was still early in the season, I was having a career year, and I figured I was worth more money than what they were offering. In this day and age, you go to the team that you think offers the best opportunity for you, not to mention the best pay. I thought I could do better, either with the Predators or with somebody else.

It turned out that I had a great season, and so did the team. We finished fourth in the Western Conference, then beat Detroit in five games in the first round of the playoffs before losing to the Phoenix Coyotes in five games in the next round. I dressed for only three playoff games, which was a real disappointment, but by then I knew my career as a Predator was coming to a close in any case. Just before the regular season ended, Poile had offered me another contract that was actually worth less money than the first offer. So there really wasn't any option. I knew that I wasn't coming back to Nashville, and that it was time to test the open market.

When the playoffs were over and Jen and I were packing up our belongings to move back to Canada for the summer, that's when it hit me. I'd spent nine years of my life in this home. But it was time for change in my life. I needed something different.

I needed new surroundings. I needed a different opportunity. It was the right thing for me to do, but it was definitely tough.

I have friends in Nashville that I'll have for life. The people there who understand the game and knew what free agency meant, they understood my position and knew that I had to go. But among the average fans, I know a lot of people were disappointed.

In the National Hockey League, July 1 is one of the most important days on the calendar. It's when players at the end of their contracts become free agents and can sign with any team. I remember being on the phone that day from about eight in the morning until four in the afternoon—conference calls with my agent and the coaches and general managers of different teams. By the time it was all finished, I think we had talked seriously with eight teams.

The Winnipeg Jets were the first team that called, just after eight, and we were on the phone with them for an hour. After that call, it got quiet and I thought, *Holy shit, maybe no one else is going to call and this will be my only opportunity.* I thought I'd love playing in Winnipeg, but at the time I didn't think going there would provide me with the best opportunity to win a Stanley Cup. But after the conversation we had with the Jets' coaching staff and management, I got off the phone and said to Jen, "Holy shit, maybe we are going to Winnipeg." They talked about their expectations for me and how they were going to help me get established in the city. It was very encouraging. The team had been back in Winnipeg for only one season at that point, and they knew that the fans would enjoy my style of play.

And, of course, it was the closet team to home—a short, direct flight from Rankin Inlet, an easy trip for my family and friends, and just down the road from where I'd played junior hockey in Brandon. If you'd asked me the day before, it would have been the last place I would have expected to wind up, but after that phone call I thought I was going to sign there for sure.

But then the phone started ringing and the calls started coming in—*boom, boom, boom, boom*—and my heart was changing every fricking hour. The Washington Capitals called. *Maybe I'm going to Washington.* I called my buddy Joel Ward to ask him about the organization. We had been neighbours in Nashville when he played for the Predators and we'd hung out quite a bit. The Flames called. *Maybe I'm going to Calgary. Do I want to play in a Canadian market?* The Florida Panthers called. That would be okay—or at least the weather would be. Things were very hectic. Not only was I talking to my agent and to the teams, but I started having conversations with players on some of the teams who were calling, asking them about the cities and about their experiences there. The day just flew by.

By the end of that afternoon, it looked like we had a deal with the New York Rangers. I really liked the idea of living in New York and playing there. My agent was just about to make a phone call to confirm the deal, but then he called me back twenty seconds after I'd hung up with him. He said that Kenny Holland, the general manager of the Detroit Red Wings, had just called, and that he'd gone over the top of what the Rangers were offering and had also thrown in a signing bonus. In my heart, I knew that I wanted to go to a contending team. I was at a point in my career when I wanted to have the best opportunity to win a Stanley Cup.

I took a look at Detroit's roster. They always seemed to be in the hunt and I thought I would be good fit there. They always made the playoffs, they had won some Stanley Cups in recent years, they had a great history, and they had great fans—I knew all about that from all the games I'd played at Joe Louis Arena with Nashville. And they didn't really have anyone who played the kind of game I did. Everything kind of happened within a couple of minutes. I felt in my heart that this was my best chance to be in the lineup every night and win a championship—and it was a bonus to go to an Original Six team with the kind of history the Red Wings have. I talked to my agent, and then we called Holland back and accepted the offer.

It was official now. I was moving on. I was a Detroit Red Wing.

Jordin had good reason to be excited about the move to the Red Wings. The Detroit organization, with general manager Ken Holland and coach Mike Babcock, was widely regarded as the gold standard in the National Hockey League. In 2013, the Wings made the playoffs for the twenty-second consecutive season, the longest active streak in the sport—and during that stretch, the team won the Stanley Cup four times. Year after year, the Wings remained in contention with a changing cast of players, but also with a strong and consistent organizational philosophy. But what they didn't have, and what they hadn't had through most of those seasons, was a player like Jordin—an agitator, an energy guy, and a fighter. His signing was seen as signal in the hockey world that Holland and Babcock felt those elements were missing from their roster, and that those elements were necessary if they were going to win another Cup. But Jordin's Detroit debut would be postponed. In the fall of 2012, for the second time in eight years, the NHL locked out its players in a labour dispute, resulting in the cancellation of training camp and the first three months of the regular season. In 2004, the previous lockout had resulted in the loss of an entire season. Jordin was still on his entry-level contract then, and so was sent down to Milwaukee in the American Hockey League, where he played the entire year. Now, as a veteran, that was no longer an option. His choices were to head for Europe, and a temporary job with a professional team there, or to wait out the lockout at home, doing his best to remain in shape. He chose the latter option.

When I signed with the Red Wings on free agency day, there was a lot of hype and a lot of excitement. I couldn't wait to get to Detroit and put on the uniform. The only guy I knew on the team was Darren Helm—he's from Winnipeg and we had crossed paths. So I called him, and I also called Zee—Henrik Zetterberg. I knew him just from playing against him for eight years. But when the lockout happened, all of that enthusiasm kind of evaporated. I stayed in Kelowna, where I lived during the off-season. There are a bunch of NHL players who spend the summers there. During the lockout, we all skated together, and some of us also practised with the local junior team, the

Kelowna Rockets of the WHL, which was great. I thought that the best thing for me was to have a home base, and know that I had ice every day and a place where I could train hard.

It was January 6 before the players finally got a deal done with the league. As soon as that happened, I made my trek to Detroit. I found a place to live out in the suburbs, and got ready for what was going to be the shortest training camp ever. I think it was only four days before we started playing games. It was a whole new experience for me, a new chapter and a fresh start. I was excited by that. But it also turned out to be a tough adjustment, and it was made that much more difficult because I had hardly any time before the regular season started. In a normal year, you would go to your city before training camp started and get used to the place and get used to the guys, and then get comfortable through camp and the exhibition season. But, because of the lockout, that didn't happen.

The Detroit players knew what I brought to the table, because we had played against each other so much, being in the same division. But because of the way I play, that meant that some of them probably didn't like me very much. I remember sitting in the dressing room during training camp and everyone was kind of silent, and then Niklas Kronwall piped up. He said, "Does anyone have anything to say to Toots after all the years of him punishing us? Now is your time to get it out, boys." I sat there quietly and thought, *Holy shit, what am I going to hear now?* But it was more of a joke and everyone just loosened up after that. Kronwall is the kind of guy who makes things easy around the dressing room and calms things down. After that moment I felt accepted by everyone, and knew that there weren't any grudges being held.

Barry Trotz had been my only NHL coach before that, and so I knew his terminology and his style inside out. When I went to Detroit, everything was new to me—not just Mike Babcock's style, but even the terms he used for everything. For nine years I was used to Trotz's meetings and having notes up on the board before the game, and then there I was in a place where they don't have meetings—they just have stuff written on a clipboard and you're on your own to figure it out. Most coaches draw up their practice drills while the players are on the ice. As players, a lot of us are still like kids. We have to be able to see information in order to process it. But Babcock would tell us about all these drills and not write anything down—just explain his drills in words and we had to process that in five seconds. I thought, *Back of the line, I go. Oh shit, I've got to remember to read all this and go over it and you never know if the coach is going to ask you a question, so you'd better know the answer. You're the new guy here, and you have to make sure you know everything.*

I admit that I was confused. Most of the other guys had been there for years. They understood Babcock's way of coaching and how things worked. I felt like I got off to bad start. Thing just happened so quickly and there was a lot of confusion. When you don't know the style of play and you're trying to adjust your game, it's extra hard if you're not sure exactly what's going on. I think, because of that, they had doubts about me right from the start, wondering whether I could play within their system.

As a professional, you have to adjust your game and your

mentality when you move to a new team, but it took me a couple of weeks to get everything down pat. I had a lot of shit to absorb in terms of getting used to the guys, getting used to the coaching style and whatnot. I knew what they'd brought me in for. There wasn't a lot of clarification during camp as to what they expected from me, but I knew what I brought to the game and I assumed that was what they needed. I played in the exhibition games and started feeling things out. Then, as the season progressed, I thought I was playing to the best of my abilities and doing what was expected of me. They seemed satisfied. They told me that they didn't need me to fight every night. They said they needed my energy and they needed me to draw penalties, and I did that. So, as far as I was concerned, everything was fine and dandy—and when things are going well for a team, everyone is happy.

I got along great with everyone in the dressing room. But it was a different kind of atmosphere. Nashville was the only NHL team I'd been with, and I guess every team has a different way of going about things. The players in Nashville were always around each other. There were a lot of team functions. You didn't just see each other at the rink. Away from the rink, guys in Nashville were hanging around a lot whereas in Detroit it was totally different. I only saw the other guys at practice and at games. So, that was a little bit of a shock to me. But I was new to the team and that was how they did things there, so I'd just have to adjust. The players kind of lived their own separate lives, and everyone lived far away from the rink. In Nashville, I lived ten minutes from the rink—in traffic. In Detroit, I was thirty minutes away without traffic. During all of that time I spent in my car, driving, I thought about a lot of stuff. When things started getting a little tough toward the end of the season, that drive seemed even longer. It was definitely hard. I put a lot of miles on my vehicle and I spent a lot of time thinking about everything that was going wrong.

It was different during games as well. The biggest thing I noticed was that the fans in Detroit really understand the game. They have a history with the sport. In Nashville, every time we touched the puck I think the fans thought we were going to score a goal. They made noise all the time. In Detroit, it was the opposite. Sometimes you could hear a pin drop out on the ice. You wouldn't have known there were twenty thousand fans in Joe Louis Arena. Regular-season hockey there is kind of blah. They know they're going to make the playoffs, so they save all of their energy for then. As it got closer to playoffs, you could feel the intensity in the arena start to build up. And then when the playoffs came around, it was like, Where were those fans all year? The raw emotion would bleed out of the stands to us.

For the first thirty-five games, I was in the lineup every night. Because of the lockout, it was a shortened season. We were playing every other day. Guys were getting injured and going in and out of the lineup. I was playing through injuries. Mentally, it was strenuous, but I kept going.

And then it just petered out from there. When I signed with Detroit, the biggest reason was because I knew there wasn't another player like me and there wasn't any question that I was going to be playing. But then I started playing fewer and fewer minutes. I was a healthy scratch on a lot of nights.

Communication is very important to me. Im guessing it's important to everyone. When you communicate, it makes things a lot easier. But I didn't find there was a lot of communication with the Red Wings. You were on your own, and you had to figure things out on your own. It's tough when you feel like you're in limbo.

I started to question myself, to ask what I wasn't doing right, what it would take for me to get back in the lineup. I started wondering about myself and doubting myself. They brought me there to bring them the physical part of the game. Then they told me I wasn't producing enough and they had to take me out of the lineup and try something new. And yet they told me that I'd done everything they'd expected.

I wanted to be in the lineup every night and I did everything I could to make that happen. When you're told you're not going to be playing, it kind of stabs you in the heart. *Should I fight more? What am I doing that's not right?* No one had any answers for me.

Then the playoffs came around. We had finished seventh in the Western Conference, just squeaking into the playoffs by a point, and were matched against the number-two seed, the Anaheim Ducks, in the first round. Obviously, they were the heavy favourites. For the first game in California, Babcock put me in the starting lineup. That made sense, because I'd played in almost every playoff game for the Predators when I was in Nashville, and they told me they were going with experience, which was a good thing for me. Then we lost, 3–1. I took a cross-checking penalty in the first period, and the Ducks scored on the power play, but otherwise I thought I had done okay. I played only a little over six minutes the entire game. No one else on the team played less than ten.

And then, the next day, my name wasn't even on the lineup sheet. When I asked why I was out, I was given the old "we're going to switch things up." And that was pretty much it. Frick, when you're told that they're going to switch things up and then they switch things up and it doesn't work, you figure you might get another chance. But after that, it was like I didn't exist. They were putting skill guys who weren't grinders on the fourth line, and all I could do was skate after practice with the other guys who hadn't dressed for the game, all the time thinking, *Geez, why the hell did I even come here?*

Players like me go to war for their teammates and do whatever it takes to be there for them. Once the playoffs come around, it's all about having a group of guys who are willing to go to war for each other. I know that I'm a guy who will do anything for his teammates. I felt I got shafted by Detroit. In my mind, it was like, *Thanks for coming out, thanks for helping us get to the playoffs, but now we're just going to go with the guys we have.* I felt like I'd fallen off the face of the earth.

We won that series with Anaheim in seven games, and then we took the Chicago Blackhawks to seven games in the second round before losing. The Hawks went on to win the Stanley Cup. But I didn't play another second after that first game against Anaheim.

After we were knocked out of the playoffs, we had a year-end team meeting. Babcock told us that if anyone wanted to meet with him individually, he could call and set something up. He said, "My phone is always on, but, otherwise, have a good summer and we'll see you in the fall." I was so furious that I just wanted to fuck off. I wanted to get out of Detroit as fast as possible. I hadn't played in a month and a half and I hadn't had any real communication with anybody in the Red Wings organization during that time. There was no way I was going to call Babcock. Why would I meet with him? What did I have to say to him—even though, deep down, I had a lot to say to him. But I thought, *Fuck it, I don't want to see him and I don't want to talk to him.*

But then I called my agent and talked to him a bit about it. I cooled off and we both decided it would better to make the call and sit down with Babcock, so I ended up having a meeting with him. And to be honest, it felt like a brush-off at the time. There isn't a hockey player in the world who doesn't want more ice time. I knew I could contribute. All my life, I've been a guy who was counted on to contribute. So it really got under my skin that Babcock didn't see things that way. But once I cooled off a little, I figured I had to try to see things his way. I realized that Babcock didn't *have* to take that meeting with me, didn't have to explain himself at all. I see now that he wasn't there to talk hockey. He just wanted to shake hands and part ways on good terms. Whatever our differences of opinion, I have to respect him for that.

And so off I went, back to Kelowna for the summer. I did my best to clear my mind and get rid of my anger. Eventually, I decided that somehow the next season would be better, that I wouldn't ask for a trade, that I would go to training camp and give it my best shot.

During the off-season, Jordin went back to Nunavut, returning to his roots, returning to the land, and shedding some of the frustration from the previous season. In addition to going home to Rankin Inlet, where he reconnected with family and friends, he embarked on what has become an annual tour of even more remote Inuit communities in Nunavut and the Northwest Territories, some of them far above the Arctic Circle. It's a way of rejuvenating himself and giving back to his people.

I have a big following in the north. How big? Well, it's hard to say. There aren't many people up there, but for those people I'm like a massive sports figure in America or maybe the president of the United States, who has millions and millions of people following him. When I fly into small communities in the north, I'm like that to them. When we're coming in, a lot of the time the pilot will make a couple of flybys to give us a bird's-eye view of how big or how small the place is. Usually there are just a few dozen houses in the middle of the tundra. From the air, you can see everyone running out of their houses and jumping on their quads or their bicycles and heading for the airport, knowing that I'm on that plane. It sends chills down my spine. It's just me. What's the big deal? Sometimes I don't get it, to be honest, because I'm just a small-town boy who grew up and was lucky enough to get to live the life that a lot of these kids wish they could live.

Visiting these communities is a way of saying thank-you for their constant loyalty and their commitment. They look up to me as a role model. They're people I can count on to be true, loyal fans, not fans of Jordin Tootoo just because he's an NHL player. They're fans because of who I am and where I grew up and the steps I've taken to be where I am today. A lot of those people have never had a chance to leave their little towns, let alone see an NHL game in person. It's an unbelievable experience for me, getting to travel across the whole of the territories. And given how the season with Detroit played out, that year's trip was especially good for me.

It's a part of the world that is very isolated from the south. Up there, you can kind of separate yourself from all of the commotion that goes on down south. These are communities of five hundred people, or three hundred people. It's very soothing for me to land in one of those places and get away from my cellphone and my other life. You're not completely cut off from the outside world, because every community is connected by the internet and has satellite television. But it's the mentality, the feeling of being apart—the same as I had growing up as a small-town boy. Life in the north is very simple. It isn't about being on a schedule. You just kind of go with the flow. I've lived in the south now for a number of years and life there gets pretty hectic. You seem to get caught up in your schedule, in what you have to do that day. In the north, it's a lot more relaxed—and it seems to get more relaxed the farther north you go.

It also does me a lot of good to go somewhere where people are real, loyal, humble, and true to themselves—where they're not fake. I'm going somewhere where I can have a heart-to-heart conversation and not have to worry about bullshitting. It seems to me that, down south, a lot of the time people tell somebody one thing and then do another. That's just how the world works sometimes. You have to bullshit your way through it. In the north, there's no bullshit. It's plain black and white. There are no grey areas. So, being in the north is a time to heal all of the wounds before I have to get back to reality. Those northern communities are the places where I feel most at home.

They also give me a chance to go back to my roots and to give back. And it's very humbling. I'm just so thankful for the support system I have in the Arctic. Any time that I can go up there and do something for the people there, I'm more than honoured to do it. I understand that I'm a huge role model. It creates an uplifting feeling in a lot of these communities to have me visit and for the kids to see their local hero. In each school I visit, we have an assembly. And then in the evenings, we have a community gathering at the local hall. I speak to everyone and say my few bits, sign autographs, and take pictures. I'm not there to preach. I'm there mainly to interact with them and say thank-you. I'm not much of a public speaker. I'd much rather sign autographs and take pictures all night than make speeches. Before I speak, I usually sit down with the mayor of the community and find out what the local issues are, and then I try to talk about them. A lot of it is about education, about convincing kids to stay in school. I also talk about community involvement, in regards to helping each other out. Pretty much every one of these communities has issues with drugs and alcohol. They know that I've been sober for three years. I talk about sobriety. I'm not a guy who is going to go out and preach about it. I try to lead by example. That's the kind of person I am. If I lead by example, hopefully a lot of these people will follow.

I understand what they're going through. I can relate. I've been there. I've seen it with my own eyes, and within my own family. Addiction. Abuse. For me to be able to speak about it and not be afraid is important, because I'm telling them not to be afraid to talk. Speak out. There's always going to be someone who is going to listen and will want to help. In these small communities, silent is the way to be. What happens behind closed doors is no one else's business. When you're in a small town and everyone knows everyone, you don't want other people knowing about your problems. People are scared to talk. People are afraid to open up. You can see it in a lot of people's eyes when I talk about situations I have experienced. I'm not directing my speeches only to the young kids; I'm directing them to the adults and the adolescents as well. I'm looking them straight in the eye, and sometimes they look away because they have experienced the same things. I need to make a point about opening up and not being afraid.

I understand now that, before I got sober, the message I was sending was pretty confused, and I wasn't setting much of an example. I was living in my own little world. I didn't understand the importance of being a role model to these people. I didn't understand how much of an influence I had in these communities, not only on the kids but also on the adults. I still made time for everybody but, mentally, I wasn't there. And I was definitely contradicting myself—talking about the importance of not drinking and then, in the evening, going out and partying it up. Discretely, I thought, but they had to notice.

When I finally figured myself out, cleaned myself up, and took a few steps back, the trips north became an unbelievable experience. Over the last three years, I've soaked so much in. To know that all of those people are behind me 100 percent is just an unbelievable feeling. When I visit those communities, every eye is watching my every move. Now that my mind is clear, I realize the effect I have on those people on a day-to-day basis. Part of my motivation for sobering up was making sure that I give myself every opportunity to have those people look up to me—because they're the ones who inspire me every day to be the best person I can be, not only for myself but as a role model in the north.

But, you know, it's not all serious. A lot of the time, girls from the communities will come up to me and ask, "Will you be my baby's daddy? Can we go on a date? Can you take me back down south?" And, obviously, I get a lot of hockey questions. I get a real chuckle out of the kids; once one kid starts asking questions, it's like a trickle effect, and suddenly they all start talking. You can see it in the kids' eyes, how excited they are. I recognize that look because I was that same kid growing up. Every time we had a guest speaker come to class, we listened and we watched. And now that guest speaker is me.

The lockout that shortened the 2012–2013 NHL season had continuing repercussions the following year. Because the regular-season schedule was reduced to forty-eight games, the league's salary *cap didn't rise to the same degree it would have following a full year of hockey. Clubs that had already committed salary through long-term contracts were going to be forced to make some difficult decisions in order to get below the threshold. Coming into training camp in the fall of 2013, everyone knew that the Red Wings, like most teams, had salary cap issues. And from the first day of camp, Jordin was one of the players on the bubble. The Wings had other options for third- and fourth-line duty, some of them earning less than the $1.9 million Jordin was guaranteed for the second year of his three-year contract. When he was hurt during training camp and missed some valuable time, the writing was on the wall, though Jordin wasn't the first to understand that.*

Going back to Detroit, I thought there was a chance it could be a whole new start for me and the Red Wings. That season, we would have a normal, full training camp, and I would have a chance to show them what I could contribute to the team. But, instead, it was the same deal right off the bat. They told me I was going to have to fight for a spot on the team. They'd signed a few guys in the off-season and there was a lot of competition for what were really just a couple of jobs.

So, deciding not to ask for a trade during the summer had kind of backfired on me. The role that I played wasn't really in their plan. They decided to go with more skilled guys throughout all four lines. I was in and out of the lineup during camp, and I felt that I did everything they asked of me. My teammates were patting me on the back and making me feel good and feel wanted on the team. But none of that mattered.

One day, I was called in and told I was being put on waivers. What that meant was that any other team in the league could claim me, but if they did, they would have to take on my contract, which I knew wasn't likely given that nearly everyone in the league was up against the salary cap. If no team claimed me, Detroit could send me down to the minors—to their American Hockey League farm team in Grand Rapids, Michigan—where they'd still have to pay me, but my salary wouldn't count against their cap. It's called "burying a contract." I wasn't the first guy it's happened to, and I won't be the last.

Kenny Holland, Detroit's general manager, gave me the news: "Toots, we have cap issues. It's unfortunate that you're the guy who has to be put on waivers. You've done everything right up to this point. You've been a real pro in the dressing room. The guys like you. Thanks for coming, but we're sending you to the minors."

Maybe I should have seen it coming, but the truth is I didn't, not at all. I knew that guys were coming back from injuries, and that there was the whole salary cap thing that the media were talking about, but it never stood out in my mind. I thought I was one of those guys they would count on. And then I got the call. They decided to go more with youth, and good for the young guys who were stepping up and seizing their opportunities. I was one of those guys not so long ago. But what happened to the part about having to earn your spot? Nowadays, everything is just kind of handed to the kids.

After I had the meeting with Holland about putting me on waivers, I called my agent. We were both really hoping that I was going to get picked up by somebody. There were teams calling about me, but nothing worked out. So I packed my bags and headed for Grand Rapids. Mentally, I wasn't ready to be in the minors. I was there physically, but I wasn't there in my head. The first couple of days, it was okay. I thought, *This is going to be temporary. I've just got to play hard and do what I do.* I was thinking, *The game is going to be a little bit easier down here, and I'm going to be faster and stronger.*

But the game in the AHL is totally different. After playing in the NHL for nine years—playing at that pace with the systems we use and the positioning of players—the truth is, in some ways it's a lot easier playing in the NHL. Down in the minors, it's kind of a mad scramble, and that wasn't good for me at that stage in my career. After the first couple of games, I was frustrated, but I kept telling myself I was just there temporarily, to let it go, to let it go. One week went by. Another week went by. By then, I was scratching my head and thinking, *Frick, somebody fucking trade me somewhere, please. I can't handle this.* Then a month had gone by and I was getting the same story every day from Detroit: *We're trying, we're doing our best. We're calling around. We're talking to teams.* And all I could think was, *Just get it done. If you have something—anything—get it done. You told me when I came here than I'm an NHL player who deserves to be in the NHL. Frick, it's been a month. What the hell is going on? Get me out of here. You guys tell me one thing and you aren't following through on it. Where's the loyalty?*

When you believe in yourself, good things are supposed to happen, but it sure didn't feel that way when I was in Grand

Rapids. I started wondering about the future. *I'm an NHL player and I deserve to be in the NHL, not the AHL. Maybe at the end of my career that's where I'll be, but I still feel like I'm in my prime.* Mentally, I was drained. I felt like I wasn't there. In terms of the people running the Red Wings, I was starting to think that since I was out of sight, I was also out of mind. It felt as though they'd tell me what I wanted to hear, and then they'd hang up and forget about me again until our next conversation.

I talked to some other guys who had been through the same experience. For example, Wade Redden—he'd been a big deal in Ottawa, a second-overall pick, an All Star; he'd played in the World Cup and then, after the 2012 lockout, he'd ended up buried in the minors just like me. Everyone I talked to said the same thing: *It's tough. You're hoping for a second chance. And you question yourself, question the decisions you made. Why the hell did I sign here when I could have signed with ten other teams?*

Finally, in December, the Red Wings had some injury problems and I was called up. I thought, *This is the opportunity I've been waiting for. This is my chance to go up there and prove that I belong.* It was a little bit strange walking back into the dressing room. When you leave and they tell the team you're not going to be around anymore, you kind of are forgotten. When I returned, I could tell the guys felt bad for my situation; I could definitely sense that. There were some awkward moments when I knew guys were wondering whether they should ask me how it had been down there. Of course, they knew I hadn't been happy in the minors.

I wound up playing only two games with the Red Wings. I

know that I had really strong games and I brought energy and physicality the way I'm supposed to. And then they sent me right back down to Grand Rapids, telling me the same stuff: "This is what we asked of you and you did it, but we're sending you back because we have guys coming off injury reserve." *Oh fuck, are you kidding me? Don't tell me what I want to hear. Just be fucking honest. I'm an honest guy, and I expect honesty in return.*

In March, the trade deadline came and went. That was really my last chance to get out of the minors during the 2013–2014 season, and I was definitely hoping for something to happen and was expecting something to happen. When nothing happened and the deadline passed, I was called into the office in Grand Rapids to talk to the head coach, Jeff Blashill. The first thing that came out of his mouth was, "How are you feeling?" *Fuck, what do you mean, how am I feeling? You know how I feel. Why are you asking me that? What do you want me to say? I'm stuck here in Grand Rapids for the rest of the year and I'm not happy about it.* Blashill understood where I was coming from. He said, "I hear you. I just want you to know I'm giving you every opportunity to get back to the NHL. You've been one of our best players ever since you came down here. You've been fighting for your life." At least that was good to hear.

What Ken Holland and Jeff Blashill couldn't have known was that I was fighting for my life in other ways. As an Inuk, I've faced racism at just about every level of the game, and I think I've got a pretty thick skin. But the things I heard in the AHL really shocked me. In four months, I had to deal with three separate incidents. That's more than during all of the time I spent in the NHL. It's bad there. Just unbelievable. With these young kids in the minors, they're undereducated and there's no sense of professionalism. They don't have respect for other players. They don't know the limits. You're supposed to let the game dictate the outcome, not personal attacks. I know there's a mental part of the game, where you try to work on guys. The type of player I am, I get under guys' skins, and I know they want to make a name for themselves by taking me on. But fuck, what I went through was just stupid, and I'm sick and tired of it.

The first time, it wasn't even one of the kids. It was Keith Aucoin, a veteran, who has logged time in the NHL. Last season he was with the Chicago Wolves, I was playing against him the whole game and frustrating him. The guy's not going to fight me. But he started waving his stick in front of me and yelling, "Go back to your fucking tribe." *Are you fucking kidding me?* The refs heard it. They kicked him out of the game. But there was no apology and really, I don't expect an apology from guys who say shit like that. I don't have time for that bullshit.

The next situation was in Milwaukee, with some nobody running around out there trying to make a name for himself, not even a real hockey player. I don't know what he was on— some kind of fucking drug or something—but right from the start of the game he was yelling and screaming at me. And then it was late in the game—three minutes left in the third period and it's tied 2-2. And he yells at me, "Go back to fucking rehab, it's where you brown people belong. . . ." Everybody heard it. The bench, the coaches and the ref. I go to the ref and say, "Are you guys hearing this fucking shit? You've got to do something."

The ref says to me, "I can't make a call like that in a 2-2 game." *Well, fuck you. Fuck you, you fucking gutless piece of shit. You've got no fucking balls.*

And then the last one was in the playoffs against Abbotsford—the second game of the first round. I wasn't even playing—I separated my shoulder in the first game, so I was scratched. At the end of the game there was a little kerfuffle on the ice. Both teams were jawing at each other, and it spilled out into the hallway in the Abbotsford arena after the game. I was just standing there by the dressing room, wearing my suit, when Abbotsford's strength and conditioning coach starts going off on one of our guys. I was watching, shaking my head. *You're a strength and conditioning coach and you're yelling at players?* Then, without me even saying a word, he starts going off on me. "Why don't you go fuck yourself. Go back to eating your fucking beluga whale, you meat head." *I looked at him and thought, really? There's no fucking room for that kind of shit.*

Everybody heard it—the Abbotsford players, our players, the security guards who were in the hallway. As soon as he said it, he turned and walked into his dressing room. I told our assistant general manager, Ryan Martin, what had happened. This shit's unbelievable, very unprofessional coming from someone on the staff. I told Ryan that it was the third time it had happened, and I didn't have time for any more apologies. I told him I was at my wit's end. I understand what it's like in the heat of the moment but fuck, there's no room for a staff member to go off on any player, never mind saying stuff like that.

A couple of days later, after the series came back to Grand

Rapids, the guy came up and apologized to me after practice. He was pretty much in tears. He said it wasn't in his personality to be like that, that he didn't know what had gotten into him. The same old story I've heard before. I just stood there and said, whatever. *Turn the page and get out of my face. You said it, and it's just uncalled for.*

The league got involved in that one, and called me to ask for my side of the story. I told them we all have to be professionals here. I understand there are kids coming out of juniors, but that doesn't make it okay. We have to be fucking adults. There has to be better education and awareness about the variety of nationalities in hockey. It doesn't matter who you are or what colour you are or what race you are. We're here to do our job.

People are cowards when it comes to personal attacks and racial comments. You saw that in the racist shit with P.K. Subban during the NHL playoffs. How bad is your life to be like that? How low can you get to be at that point?

Whenever I speak to groups of young people when I am back home, I stress that if I could make it, they can make it. So when some racist clown starts yapping, it's not so much that he is getting under my skin, it's that he is making it clear that he would make life more difficult for all those kids I speak to and try to encourage. Look, I can take care of myself. And if someone really wants to call me out, they don't need to be racist to do it. But if you use that kind of language around me, that's not just a personal attack. That's an attack on a whole people. You can't just sweep that under the rug, or say sorry and expect it to go away.

But obviously I can't blame the Red Wings for the behaviour of the opposition in the AHL. Putting on the Red Wings jersey for the first time is a memory I'll have forever. Playing for an Original Six team has been one of the highlights of my career. The fan following that the Red Wings have throughout North America is unbelievable, and I was a part of that. But hockey is a job, and sometimes not being in control of your own destiny is part of it, too. I know I can still play in the NHL. I can't go back in time and wonder why I signed with Detroit. With new beginnings, you take your chances. I thought signing with Detroit was my best opportunity to be in the lineup every night. But it wasn't. And I just have to be grateful for every opportunity that I had to play with them, and try to accept that things just didn't work out.

Hopefully, somewhere down the line, my name will come up and someone will trade for me in the off-season. Unless someone believes in you, you've got no chance. I'm just waiting for that one opportunity where someone believes in me and knows that I can play. And in the meantime, it's about being professional. And I'm grateful that I still get to play this game.

This experience will make me a stronger person and build more character that will help me fight through adversity. I've been through a lot in my life, but in the hockey business you have to understand that everything isn't always fine and dandy. Even if you're in the NHL, it doesn't mean that life is always great. It's one thing to make it to the NHL and it's another thing to stay in the NHL. Playing in the minors is a test of my willpower, a chance for me to be mentally strong and believe in myself, and I'm going to pass the test.

It is summer in Rankin Inlet again, the short season of long days when Jordin returns home. It is a chance to go out on the land, to hunt and fish with his dad, Barney, and his nephews, to reconnect with his family and friends and his people, to shed the frustrations of life in the south, to forget—and to remember.

As a kid, life in the Arctic was all I knew. I grew up in a community with no high-rise buildings, with not a lot of vehicles around, and with no roads past the edge of town. That was normal to me. Driving around on a Ski-Doo was the most amazing thing you could do, and any time my dad got a new snowmobile or built a new sled for hunting, it was as if that was a limousine. When I go home in the summer, I send pictures to my friends—and hockey players know all about limousines and expensive sports cars. I'll send them a picture of a Ski-Doo or a quad with a sled or trailer on the back, with a note saying, *This is my limousine.* They all get a chuckle out of it. Materialistic things just don't matter in the north. You look at kids down south and they know all about Maseratis and Bentleys and Range Rovers. The kids up north might see those things on television, but they just don't matter to them. They didn't matter to me as a kid and they still don't as an adult. I've worked hard all my life, and I feel like I deserve things that will make me happy, but for me it's more important to have hunting gear or a fishing pole.

When I go home, no one treats me any differently than they

did before I made it in hockey. That speaks volumes about our people. I just want to be treated as the Jordin who grew up there. I don't expect any higher praise or anything like that. The people in my community, in all of Nunavut, are regular folks. That's in our blood and in our nature. You treat everyone else as you want to be treated. I love going home because I can enjoy life without people coming up to me and wanting to be my friend just because I play in the NHL.

It has been a long, tough journey from a small town in Nunavut to where I am now, and so far I'm the only one who has made it. I always tell myself that I'm just paving the way for the next young Inuk to come along and say, *If he can do it, I can do it.* It doesn't matter where you come from. The mental and physical battles I endured growing up only led to bigger and better things. They prepared me for life. I dealt with a lot of family issues along the way but, looking back, I think that everyone has family issues and that I enjoyed a pretty good childhood. I look back on the hunting trips, the fishing derbies we all went out on together, the camping. Those are things not a lot of kids get to experience nowadays.

I wouldn't take back anything that has happened to me in the past. It all happened and some of it was terrible. But it was a building block. I don't hold a grudge against anyone who has done harm to me. Every individual takes a different path. My childhood and my teenage years have made me into the person I am today. I'm glad I got to face those hard times and experience all of those hardships. And in the end, I have to thank my parents. I love them to death. I can't speak highly enough of them. I know that might seem strange to people, now that they have read about some of the things my parents put us through, but I still believe that they're the greatest people I know. They have their own struggles and problems. I get that. I didn't get that as a kid, but I do now. And there are experiences I've had with them—both good and bad—that I'm never going to forget. You've got to take that and learn from it.

In the end, I found a way to believe in myself. I learned to never give up. It's been embedded in my heart ever since I was a fricking kid. I was always told I was too small and was never going to make it to the big leagues. But I had that drive, that motivation. It's always been there. There were times when I wondered why. It took me years to realize that I was trying to prove something to others—and to myself. I wanted to show the whole damn world that it doesn't matter what other people think. If you put your mind to it, the sky's the limit. I've battled all my life. And I'm not about to stop now.

The difference is that I've become comfortable in my own skin. I'm true to myself, and I'm true to the people I love. I don't use anything to hide anymore. This is me now. I'm just trying to lead by example and show everyone who ever doubted me. I'm going to do that by being honest with myself, first and foremost. I've said a lot of shit to a lot of people that I didn't follow through on, because I thought I had better things to do—including partying to fill the void after Terence died. Now I can go to bed at night with no problem and not have a million things running through my mind.

But I dream of him. I dream of him all the time.

It's weird. The dreams are usually about stuff we used to do. Like when we were out on the land, camping. In one dream, right before I wake up, he's on our boat and I'm on land, and he's kind of motoring away. I'm stuck on the land and he's going off into his own world. I've had that dream on more than one occasion.

In another dream, we are walking around in a mall. I jump on the escalator and he stays at the bottom, and while I'm going up and away from him, he says, "Jordin, you can go your own way now."

Or we'll be walking down a street and I'll turn a corner and he'll just stop there. I'll say, "Come on, let's go. What are you doing?" And he'll wave at me and say, "Go ahead. Go ahead."

And then there is the one where we are out skydiving and we jump out of the plane together and we're holding hands and then he lets my hand go and we float away from each other. We're always going our separate ways before I wake up.

I'm not frightened by those dreams. I actually wish that they would happen more often, so that Terence and I could relive the good times we had together. I wake up and say, "Are you here?" Jennifer will ask me if I'm okay, and then I'll tell her about the dream. She never met my brother, and I wish she could experience how I feel after those dreams.

It feels like Terence is still somewhere out there, like he ran away but he's still somewhere in this world.

INDEX

INDEX

INDEX

INDEX